✧ ✧ ✧

Endorsements

"Sharon Lund, through exploring 18 near-death cases, gives us a moving and heartfelt picture of not only what the experiencers went through but vivid portrayals of the afterlife. The reality of what happens to us after we die opens up here in ways anyone can connect with.

"Informative material on the phenomenon of near-death itself is covered, along with what is typical for experiencers in dealing with life-changing aftereffects. Thank you, Sharon, for sharing the results with us of your continued dedication to help, to heal, and to teach."
—P.M.H. Atwater, LHD
Researcher and author of numerous books about her findings, including *The Big Book of Near-Death Experiences* and *Near-Death Experiences: The Rest of the Story* (due out 1/2011)

"Who better to trust about the realities of the death experience than someone who has experienced it directly? In There Is More . . . 18 Near-Death Experiences, Sharon Lund generously shares the wisdom, compassion, and fearlessness that evolved through her near-death experiences. With tremendous heart, Sharon gives us compassionate comfort along with a fierce reminder that death is actually undying aliveness, that death is not the enemy of life but its radiant complement.

"Sharon's calling is not only to lovingly support those who are facing death, but also those who face life with fear and

anxiety. Her vital message is for everyone because it redefines living. I'm using There Is More . . . 18 Near-Death Experiences, as well as Sharon's award-winning documentary Dying to LIVE: NDE, as teaching tools in my spiritual community. They keep fresh the reality of death as a divine doorway to radical aliveness."
—Michael Bernard Beckwith
Founder Spiritual Director
Agape International Spiritual Center

"The taboo on confronting death in our culture has been broken, and Sharon Lund is one of the most important taboo breakers. The wisdom embodied in the experiences of the diverse individuals in this book is revealing, inspiring, and fulfilling. There Is More…18 Near-Death Experiences is a major contribution. If you need a dose of hope in confronting your mortality, this book is for you."
—Larry Dossey, MD
Author of The Power of Premonitions: How Knowing the Future Shapes Our Lives

"Rev. Dr. Sharon Lund, takes us deeper into who we are on the ultimate journey of dying and death, and comes back renewed. Inspired by these amazing 18 near-death experiences, our lives become richer and more meaningful as we understand how we are all connected and the love that is within each person and every thing."
—Stephen and Ondrea Levine
Authors of A Year to Live: How to Live This Year As If It Were Your Last; Who Dies: An Investigation of Conscious Living and Conscious Dying

"Out of the ashes of a shattered life, Sharon Lund has the courage to turn tragedy into lessons of unconditional love and peace—the touching and ultimate reality on earth. We truly are more than this reality!"
—Jeffrey Long, MD
Author of *Evidence of Afterlife: The Science of Near-Death Experiences*
—Jody Long, JD
Author of *From Soul to Soulmate: Bridges from Near-Death Experience Wisdom*

"As a professional counselor for the past 29 years, I have been honored to join with countless people in their journeys through the intense pain of grief. Rev. Dr. Sharon Lund's book There Is More . . . 18 Near-Death Experiences, *like her documentary* Dying to LIVE: NDE, *can bring the gift of hope not only to a dying person, but as members of my VITAS bereavement writing group expressed after viewing the film, it can give precious unexpected hope and comfort to someone overwhelmed with grief.*"
—LaVon Switzer, LCSW
Bereavement Services Manager
VITAS Innovative Hospice Care

✧ ✧ ✧

There Is More . . .

✧ ✧ ✧

There Is More . . .

18 Near-Death Experiences

Sharon Lund, DD

with

Monica Hagen and Hector Keaopā'uhane

✧ ✧ ✧
THERE IS MORE...
18 Near-Death Experiences

Copyright © 2010 by Sharon Lund, DD

All rights reserved. No part of this book may be used or reproduced by any means, graphic, electronic, or mechanical, including photocopying, recording, taping, or by any information storage retrieval system without the written permission of the publisher except in the case of brief quotations embodied in critical articles and reviews.

THERE IS MORE: 18 Near-Death Experiences may be purchased or ordered through booksellers or at SacredLife.com.

ISBN: 0-9822331-3-2
ISBN: 978-0-9822331-3-9
Library of Congress Control Number: 2010909361

The information, ideas, and suggestions in this book are not intended as a substitute for professional advice. Before following any suggestions contained in this book, consult your physician or mental health professional. Neither the author nor the publisher shall be liable or responsible for any loss or damage allegedly arising as a consequence of your use or application of any information or suggestions in this book.

Cover and text design: Miko Radcliffe at drawingacrowd.net
Cover photo: "Girl Scout Poetry" NASAImages.org
Photo of Sharon Lund: Jeaneen Lund at jeaneenlund.com

Sacred Life Publishers™
SacredLife.com
Printed in the United States of America

Contents

Introduction xiii

✧

Childhood Experiences

Childhood Experiences 3

Sharon (Clark) Lund, DD – Raped 5

Nikki – Emotional Trauma 11

Bernie Siegel, MD – Choked on a Toy 19

Tessa – Overwhelmed 25

✧

Adolescent Experiences

Dominique – Repeatedly Abused 35

Colter Rios – Paralyzed from a Football Injury 45

Adult Experiences

Sharon Lund, DD – Suicide Attempts
and AIDS Complications 51

Nancy Maier – Fell Off Ladder.. 65

John Burchard – Heart Attack.. 73

Alexis Burris – Pneumonia 77

Jil Streed – Trapped in Wildfire.. 83

Dan Schaff – MRSA (Staph Infection)..................................... 89

Carla Jean Tooker – Diabetic Coma 97

Helen Wendle – Suicide Attempt 101

Scott Borowik – Car Accident 109

Vanessa Chicca – Domestic Violence 119

Tianna Conte, PhD – Heat-Induced Heart Failure.................... 125

✧ ✧ ✧

The Common Thread 131

Heartfelt Love and Appreciation 137

My Amazing Project Team... 139

✧ ✧ ✧

Appendix

Frequently Asked Questions 143

Verifying a Near-Death Experience.. 159

Definitions of an NDE, OBE, dNDE 162

Characteristics of a Near-Death Experience 164

What Changes Typically Occur in Children
    Following a Near-Death Experience? 167

What are the Phases of Adjustment
    after a Childhood Near-Death Experience?....................... 169

How Can Caregivers Help a Childhood NDEr? 170

Support and Resources
    for NDEs, dNDEs, OBEs, STEs.. 172

Other Support and Resources... 175

Recommended Books by International Association of Near-
Death Studies (IANDS).. 182

Other Valuable Books and DVDs 184

Introduction

"It's only when we truly know and understand that we have a limited time on Earth – and that we have no way of knowing when our time is up, we will then begin to live each day to the fullest, as if it was the only one we had."
~ Elisabeth Kübler-Ross[1]

Open your heart and mind and journey with me to embrace life and death in a very sacred way.

My name is Sharon Lund. I have danced with life and death through six decades on this planet, overcoming nine years of childhood sexual abuse, suicide attempts, anorexia, destructive relationships, HIV/AIDS since 1983, and near-death experiences.

I consider all my challenges to be blessings because each obstacle seeded a gift. These blessings allowed me to heal, discover more of who I am, and become whole. I embrace who I am today, living my life's purpose with passion and love. I learned that it's not what happens in life but how you react to it that's important.

Death is a subject few people feel comfortable talking about, yet it's one thing everyone has in common. Why do so many people fear dying and death? Because they believe in Hell? Because they fear the unknown? Because they fear pain and suffering, lack of control, or separation from loved ones?

---

[1] For information about Elisabeth Kübler-Ross, please go to elisabethkublerross.com or ekrfoundation.org.

There Is More . . .

What if dying and death are catalysts to life? What if life only consists of changing expressions of ourselves? What if death is a change of focus of our consciousness, from one plane to another?

Since 1986, I have helped men, women, and children prepare for their transitions (deaths) and have sat at their bedsides as they journeyed into the next phase of their Being. This is one of the greatest gifts I have received—being with them as they made their transitions.

I also assisted people in preparing their legacies, and creating a unique memorials or celebrations before making their transitions. Using the questions from my book *Scared Living, Sacred Dying: A Guide to Embracing Life and Death*, I've repeatedly witnessed that people who actually face death start to live their lives more fully. They get their affairs in order; some quit jobs they hate and start doing what fulfills their hearts and souls, many leave relationships that haven't worked, while others become committed to relationships they took for granted.

When we realize we don't know when our last breath of life will be, we truly embrace each moment and express ourselves with more gratitude and love, and sometimes it leads to unexpected places.

In 2009, I published my second book, *The Integrated Being: Techniques to Heal Your Mind-Body-Spirit.* Shortly after celebrating the birth of this book, I asked God to inform me of my next step by stating, "Infinite Spirit, I surrender my will and let you guide me." What I heard was, "It is time for you to produce a documentary on near-death experiences."

In many ways, I was surprised because I had never created a documentary before. Yet I knew I would be Divinely guided and this work was out of my hands. I became the expression of God working through me.

Introduction

Every step of the way came with ease, grace, and love. Our production team was gifted with equipment for two months, all the people we interviewed came to us with ease, and we witnessed miracles. We wrapped up filming our documentary, *Dying to LIVE: NDE,* in two months. Four months later, we premiered our movie to an audience of 383 people. We set aside our egos and allowed the Universe to flow through us.

We received outstanding endorsements for this documentary from Michael Bernard Beckwith, Larry Dossey, MD, Stephen and Ondrea Levine, Bernie Siegel, MD, and others. On April 25, 2010, we received the Silver Lei Award from the Honolulu International Film Festival.

After our documentary was released, we were guided to our next project, this book, which includes ten extended interviews from our documentary as well as new interviews.

In this book, the interviews were conducted by Monica Hagen, Hector Keaopā'uhane and me. For clarity, I state that I am the interviewer. However, without Monica and Hector, the stories would not be complete. They are my Earth angels! After each interview I share more information about the person and their current status. Then, in italics, I share my insights and thoughts about their NDEs and what led up to them.

Within these interviews, you will discover that regardless of whether a person has had an incredible or a distressful NDE, their experience is "more real than real." In fact, it's the most powerful event of their lives because it transforms who they are and how they see the world. It usually eliminated their fear of death.

It was extremely difficult for those interviewed to find words to describe their experiences. After a powerful, life-changing NDE, most people accept death as part of their unfolding process. They understand the sacredness, love, and Oneness of everything and everyone.

Many people have experienced the feelings and emotions of NDEs without being close to death themselves through meditation, prayer, experiencing deep emotional stress, or being present with a dying person or beloved pet. Within the pages of this book, you have an opportunity to release fear, embrace the sacred cycle of life, death, and understand the healing and immense love that surrounds death.

You may read this book out of curiosity or to dispel fear. You also may want to gain insight into your own near-death experience (NDE), out-of-body experience (OBE), distressing near-death experience (dNDE), or spiritual transformative experience (STE). Some experiences may even be blocked memories, only to come forward later, triggered when it becomes safe to explore those emotions.

Millions of people around the world—men, women, and children like you and me—have had near-death experiences (NDEs). We bring the messages that when people die, they are immediately healed. They feel peace, tranquility, and they experience a greater love than they have ever known in this lifetime.

Through the stories in *There Is More . . . 18 Near-Death Experiences,* I believe you'll discover hope, love, and a deeper understanding of yourself and the Oneness of All.

Love and Blessings,

Sharon

Sharon Lund, DD

Childhood Experiences

✦
Childhood Experiences

Some children who have near-death experiences either don't recall them or block the memories of the events that triggered their NDEs, such as a difficult birth, an illness, stress or abuse.

P.M.H. Atwater, author of the books *The New Children and Near-Death Experiences* and *The Big Book on Near-Death Experiences*, states, "Children will 'tuck away' in their minds anything that is not useable in their world. If something conflicts with their need to grow and learn, they will either repress it or just 'forget about it for now.' That's why it is critically important to educate parents to listen to their children and *not* criticize them for 'fanciful tales' after nearly dying or being seriously ill.

"The average child experiencer takes at least 20 to 30 years to integrate their experiences, some more. Children do not 'connect the dots' while maturing; they are not aware that their various 'differences' are normal for what they went through when young; they are not something to make excuses for or deny."

P.M.H. also states, "With children, I found that 61% regret having had their near-death experience afterward. It caused them many incidents of embarrassment, discomfort, and confusion. They did not 'fit in' with their peer group afterward, nor with their families, even to the point of feeling 'foreign'—as if they no longer belonged."

Child experiencers may demonstrate some of the following characteristics after the event: advanced maturity, increased psychic abilities, seeing auras, recall seeing the Light, remembering an out-of-body experience, communicating with

There Is More . . .

spirits/angels/guides, feeling Universal Love for everything and everyone, and increased interest in serving others.

If your child or anyone you know shows signs of an NDE, assist them with your understanding, encouragement, and support.

Sharon (Clark) Lund, DD
Raped

As far back as I remember, I loved being a mommy to all of my baby dolls, especially Susie. Susie was a Madame Alexandra doll with long, curly brown hair, big dark eyes, cloth body, and soft rubber skin. I cared for Susie like any mother would care for the child she dearly loved.

I told Susie everything, even when I heard over and over throughout the years, *"If you tell anyone, I will kill your mommy."* Telling Susie seemed safe. She would keep my secret and share my burden.

From the age of three until twelve years old, whenever my family visited my grandfather, he raped me.

I crossed my arms tight and yelled, "NO!" Then I stomped my feet. My voice quivered as I shouted, "I don't want to go! Don't take me there! Please don't make me go! Can't we please, please, please go to the zoo?" I loved to watch the animals play, especially the monkeys. The mother always protected her baby. She held it close to her chest, swung with it, and kissed her little one. The big monkeys watched over the small ones and made sure they didn't get hurt.

I wish Mommy and Daddy would protect me!

Daddy said, "We can't go to the zoo today. We have to visit your grandma and grandpa."

There Is More . . .

That was the last place I wanted to go. My body trembled and my tummy felt like it had butterflies in it. Instead of going to a fun place, we were going to a bad one!

Why would anyone want to visit my daddy's parents at their home?

Grandpa was really mean! He yelled at Grandma, Daddy, Mommy, Tommy, me, anyone who was around. He told everyone what to do and we had to mind him. I never saw him happy.

I hated Grandpa! My parents told me not to hate anyone, but I couldn't help it. I did hate him!

Soon after we arrived at their house, Grandma called me. "Sharon, come down here. Go help your grandpa pick some jams and canned vegetables for dinner."

Those were the same words I always heard when we visited them. I ducked behind the bed and shouted, "No, Grandma! I don't want to."

I heard Grandpa's mean voice yell, "Mind your grandmother and come with me right now!"

My eyes filled with tears as I walked slowly into the living room. No one noticed me. Mommy and Daddy played a board game. Tommy sat by the window, probably watching a fisherman in a boat. They had no idea where they were sending me.

My body stiffened. Grandpa's rough, smoke-stained fingers grabbed my hand. It hurt! I tried to squirm away, but he held on tighter.

As he walked me out of the house and dragged me to the cellar, I felt cold. I shivered. He swung open the squeaky door and rushed me past Grandma's preserves. Then he pulled me to his workbench in the far corner. I knew this area well! This was where he hurt me. I silently screamed over and over. I wondered, "Doesn't anyone know he's going to hurt me again?" I told myself to run away, but I couldn't.

Grandpa lifted me onto his cold, hard workbench. He smiled and said with his stinky breath, "Sharon, you look so pretty today." Then he kissed my neck. I shook so hard my body flopped around like Jell-O. He quickly raised my beautiful dress and pulled off my ruffled panties. His deep voice said what I didn't want to hear, "I love you, Sharon."

I tried to push his hand away, but he yelled, "Don't you dare do that! Sit on your hands right now!"

I sat on top of them and hurt my fingers. I wanted to hit him, but I couldn't move my hands.

Mommy and Daddy told me to mind my elders, but I didn't want to mind Grandpa. I didn't want to get hurt again.

Tears filled my eyes. I begged, "No, Grandpa! Don't do that!"

He shouted, "Sharon, shut up! Open your legs wider. You'll be sorry if you don't!"

My body tightened. "No! No! Leave me alone!"

He grabbed a sock that was always on the workbench. He stuffed part of it into my mouth. It was dry and it hurt me. No words could come out, yet my mute voice screamed for help. In my mind I prayed, "God, please help me! Don't let my grandpa do this to me again. Someone help me! Please!"

There Is More . . .

In a mean voice, Grandpa whispered, "Remember, if you tell anyone, I will kill your mommy!"

I knew I couldn't tell anyone what he did to me. I had to keep it a secret! I needed to save Mommy's life!

Then my BEAUTIFUL angel, Laura, came to me as she had before. Sometimes I could see through her. She wore a long pink gown. She had crystal blue eyes and long curly blonde hair.

Whenever Grandpa hurt me, Laura lifted me out of my body and took me away from him and the cellar. We'd go to fun places, like to the park to swing. When I was way up high, I tried to reach out and touch the clouds. Sometimes we'd go to the beach and I would play in the sand or watch the seagulls.

Laura told me if I stayed very quiet, everything in the world would speak to me. Sometimes plants, animals, and even rocks talked to me. At the park, trees and flowers told me when they wanted more sun. Some said they needed to be moved—they had trouble breathing and growing where they were located. Laura said, "We are all connected."

She also told me that whenever I was frightened or in pain, if I took a lot of deep, deep breaths, that would calm me.

Most of all I liked it when Laura took me to my favorite place in the whole world, my Special Room in my parents' house. I reeeeally liked it when she took me there. I played with Laura and Susie and all my baby dolls. I felt safe there!

When we were through playing, Laura told me she loved me. I liked to hear her tell me that, but I didn't like it when Grandpa said he loved me. Before she left, I silently said, "Laura, I love you!" Then we hugged and kissed each other goodbye. She suddenly whisked away into the air. I felt sad when she left, but I knew she'd return.

I opened my eyes wide when I felt Grandpa put my panties back on me. He pulled the sock out of my mouth. "You're a good girl, Sharon."

Tears flowed down my face and into my mouth. As I licked my salty tears, Grandpa pounded his huge fist on the bench and yelled, "Stop crying! Right now!" He roughly wiped my tears with the sock, then lifted me off his workbench. My body shook inside and out. I hurt like I was on fire. I wished I could make the hurt go away.

Before leaving, Grandpa grabbed jars of vegetables and jams. He didn't even let me pick them out. After we stepped outside the cold cellar, he slammed the door shut. He no longer gripped my hand, as he'd taken what he wanted!

Grandpa hurried back to the house ahead of me. Then he waited for me on the porch and said again in a mean voice, "If you tell anyone, I'll kill your mommy."

When I was older, my grandfather made me do sexual things to him. I prayed every night for him to die. When I was twelve years old he did. I blamed myself—guilt and shame ate me up.

At a young age, I knew in my heart I wanted to be a mommy of a baby girl, nurse, teacher, and a nun when I grew up. In a way, all of these happened, just differently than I expected. I am a mother of a beautiful daughter, Jeaneen. I helped nurse AIDS patients and others, I teach spiritual lessons, and I'm a New Thought Minister.

There Is More . . .

Millions of children around the world have been—and will continue to be—sexually abused. What I now realize is the importance of telling someone—parents, teacher, clergy, friend. Say what happened until someone believes you.

Abuse has to stop, but it can only stop when those being abused break their silence. Silence can kill, emotionally, mentally and physically. (Because of my silence, I became anorexic and suicidal.)

All aspects of our lives are affected by secrets. Like a festering sore, secrets wear us down until we either admit the abuse to a concerned person or hurt ourselves or others (expressed as rage, depression, or compulsive behavior).

When my grandfather raped me, my Spirit was lifted out of my body so I wouldn't have to endure the physical pain in the moment. Still, I felt the aftereffects especially because of the secrecy. I understand now how our Spirits can endure a lot and God will never give me more than I can handle. I just wish I had felt able to tell someone at the time.

The blessing I received was my deep connection to my Angel of Love, Laura, and the opportunity to communicate with the various kingdoms (plant, mineral, animal, human, and Spirit) from a place of Oneness and Love. At a young age, I realized there is no separation, that we are all magnificent Beings of Light, Love, and Oneness.

You can attain that connection without having to endure abuse. However, if abuse is part of your past, you can use that experience to springboard forward, perhaps by helping others or simply by being gentler with yourself.

Nikki
Emotional Trauma

Mature beyond her years, twelve-year-old Nikki is wise, smart, humorous, and bubbly. Her blonde hair outlines her round face and her long eyelashes frame her beautiful blue eyes.

"I started having out-of-body experiences when I was three years old," she said. "I heard my mom choking to death and I was scared. I remember a black shadow came to me and then, POOF! I was floating out of my body. I didn't know I was actually out of it, but I floated to my mother's bedroom and made sure she was okay. After that, every night, I woke up and checked on my mother to make sure she was still breathing."

Nikki still sounds sad when she speaks of her first six years with her biological parents. "My childhood was so rough, you can't even imagine. When I think of my mother, I get sad because she's on drugs and doesn't make the right choices. I love her, but I'm scared for her because she could die from drugs and danger."

Nikki hadn't seen her birth mom in several years until they both attended a relative's funeral in September 2009. "I cried the entire time when I saw my birth mom. Just knowing she's alive, I kept saying, *thank you, thank you.*"

Nikki's parents fought every day. "My mom wasn't someone you would choose as a parent." Her parents went their separate ways when she was an infant. However, for several years, Nikki bounced back and forth between them.

There Is More . . .

Her dad had a lot of different girlfriends. For awhile, he dated a woman she didn't care for.

"I didn't like that lady at all. She was like the evil stepmother from Cinderella. She made me do things I didn't want to do, but I didn't have the courage to tell my dad. While he worked every day, she had a full day to be mean to me. She hit me for no reason and spanked me with a belt until I was entirely red. Then when my dad came home, she acted like the perfect person."

Living in that environment made it hard for Nikki to get a good night's rest. "When I don't sleep, my head doesn't work well. Sometimes I can't even count numbers. The only time I had peace and quiet was at school."

Nikki moved in with her new mom (her dad's former nice girlfriend) at six years old. This woman loved the girl the moment she saw her and embraced her like her own daughter. She became Nikki's guardian because her dad and evil girlfriend could no longer care for her.

"My life with my new mom is like being granted my wish. My life is beautiful—I love it now and I wouldn't trade it for anything. I have the little sister I've always wanted. I got my wish granted to me—*a better life.*"

Nikki had her near-death experience while in kindergarten.

"I was on a real big metal slide at school when I got dizzy and fell to the ground. I was knocked out and saw a tiny bit of my past, all the meanness, fighting, and anger in my family. I journeyed through my own little world and saw the Light. Spirits stood all around me and looked at me. I knew I wasn't ready to go yet. I still had a full life to live." When she finally opened her eyes, she saw her classmates and teacher looking her over to make sure she was all right. Since that day, Nikki's life changed. She now sees Spirits and auras.

"The first time I saw Spirits, I was six years old and living with my current, wonderful mom. I was sleeping in my bed and I saw a figure in white. I had my nightlight on because I don't like the dark. I looked at the figure and then it was gone. I ran crying to my mom. I didn't know how to explain what happened because I was too little," she said.

"When I was younger, I talked to myself and the Spirits. My mom couldn't see them. I could only see little parts of the Spirits, but I knew what they were."

Ever since Nikki fell, she also saw Spirits of dead relatives and people she didn't know. "Not long ago, Grandpa passed away. I didn't get to spend much time with him, but I felt really close to him and liked to be with him. When he was alive, he liked NASCAR races.

"One day, my new mom and I were sitting on the couch watching the races. I kept looking over to the end of the couch where I saw my dead grandpa. He sat there with us and we asked him questions, but he didn't answer. He just watched the race. I knew it was him—I could see the shape of his head. After he died, he turned into Light."

Nikki remembered her mom driving her to the park one day and they both saw the Spirit of her grandpa riding in the car with them. "First I felt a slight breeze on the back of my neck, but the windows were closed. I felt it again and Mom told me it was probably the wind rushing in. But Grandpa was in the back seat, just checking out where we were going. He looked a lot younger than I remember him, only twenty or thirty years old."

There Is More . . .

Nikki is not frightened of the Spirits she sees because she can tell if they are good or bad by their auras. "I can see auras for one or two minutes. They show me when a Spirit is around and if the aura is dark, I know it's negative or bad. If it's white like my mom's, I know it's a good Spirit.

"I've seen auras as long as I can remember, back to when I had the accident on the slide. One day at school, a girl I didn't like came toward me and I saw that her aura was black. She was later suspended from school. Black means bad and negative. We don't want to be around that kind of person.

"I love seeing the aura of one of my friends at school—it's bright white and perky like my mom's.

"Usually, my senses are really strong. Colors are bright and I see things a lot of people don't."

Nikki sees Spirits at least twice per week, often in one corner of her bedroom. "A few weeks ago, during the night, I noticed a dark figure up in the top corner of the room. Then it disappeared. I was a little scared because it wasn't good energy.

"Last night I saw one in the same area again, and it just sat there and looked around. This one didn't scare me. I was curious what it wanted from me. Tonight at six o'clock, there was a Spirit here in my mom's room. He looked at my mom and then went away."

She can tell when Spirits have darkness around them, "But I also saw a little bit of light above their heads. They float and come toward me. I wish I knew who they were or why they come to me."

I asked Nikki how she reacts or responds when she sees a Spirit. "I stay calm and look at it. I can feel what it feels." She told me she doesn't share any of these visions with her friends. "I keep them to myself and my family because some people won't understand. They might think I should go to the loony bin."

Several times a week, she dreams that her Spirit lifts out of her body. Sometimes these dreams are good and other times she wakes up frightened.

Nikki shared what it's like getting older. "I'm getting an attitude and putting blame on others. I still have some of that meanness in me—for some reason I can't get that out. It's impossible. I do a lot of back talking to the teachers. I can beat a fourteen-year-old boy in wrestling. I've grown up to be so strong because I had to protect and defend myself as a child. I had to learn to fight.

"I can be the nicest person in the world, but if someone hits me or gets mad at me, I start fighting hard. I use my full strength and that person ends up losing. My dad taught me how to fight and stand up for myself. As a child, I learned how to shoot a gun and how to fight to keep alive.

"My birth mother gave me the attitude."

Nikki repeated several times that her past was all about fighting. "Before being with my dad's evil girlfriend, I was a normal kid with a normal life—but tough. Now, I'm kind of a tomboy."

Nikki believes her visions are gifts. "I think seeing auras and Spirits was a gift from Heaven to see what's good and bad.

"For fun, I like to swim, go to the movies, roller skate, play tag and hide-and-go-seek, and spend time with my family and friends."

I asked Nikki if she wanted to share anything else. "Mom and I invite the good things into our lives every day. We have certain rituals and prayers, but we don't go to church. Some churches are fear-based. God is real, God is good. End of story."

She giggled and added, "Oh, yeah. I went on a shamanic journey the other day and got in touch with my animal totem, which is an eagle. The eagle told me his name. I'm going back again to connect with my guides. Recently I've been able to tap into people's past lives."

I heard excitement in Nikki's voice.

"We were at my mom's friend's house, and I noticed that with one of the women, I could see her past. She was five or six years old and it was during a war. The little girl was frightened and she had to go down to the cellar to be protected. I didn't tell the lady what I saw because I didn't know her. It's really cool to see different things, but I'm not sure how I'm going to handle it. My mom and I are going to look for direction."

She laughed, "I'm happy!"

Nikki wants to become a veterinarian. "I'm really good with animals. Every kind of animal likes me. When I talk to them, they know what I'm saying. I have a parakeet, Buddie. When I talk to him, he listens, and when I'm finished, he talks back to me."

Despite all that Nikki experienced at a young age, she still has an enduring sense of humor and desire to seek the truth. She is a warrior.

Nikki

Nikki was so connected to her birth mother that when her mother was being abused, Nikki's Spirit lifted out of her body to aide and protect her. Afterward, Nikki acted as her mother's protector, checking on her regularly. This is a large burden for a child, but one she took on willingly.

Thankfully, that daily burden of being her mother's keeper has been lifted. Now Nikki lives a good life with a mother who truly loves her and allows her to live without fear.

Nikki welcomes her psychic gifts, including seeing auras that allow her to determine good from bad, witnessing Spirits, and tapping into the energy of her totem animal. She is a seeker and is blessed by her new mother who encourages Nikki to expand her gifts and use them for the well-being of herself and others.

You have these gifts as well. Quiet your mind and access Divine wisdom within you.

Bernie Siegel, MD
Choked on a Toy

As a child, Bernie—today a famous doctor and author—was bright, loved art, and did a little of everything. He grew up in New York and during the summers, he enjoyed playing outside with everyone. The neighborhood was like family, and someone's religion or color didn't matter.

"I had a good life and a lot of people loved me. I had wonderful grandparents. I was born an ugly duckling because my birth was delayed. When they handed me to my mother, she said they handed her a purple melon, not a child. My grandparents accepted me as I was. In fact, my grandma massaged me five to six times a day to push things back where they belonged. As an adult, I know the importance of her touch and massage."

Bernie chokes up whenever he thinks or talks about his NDE. "As a four year old, I was home with an ear infection, sitting on the end of the bed. My mother was pregnant at the time and in the kitchen. I had a toy telephone and had seen carpenters put nails in their mouths and then spit them out one at a time as they needed them. So I unscrewed the dial and put all the small pieces in my mouth. When I breathed in, they went into my throat and I felt the most pain I'd ever experienced. My body went into a spasm and I couldn't talk or call for help.

"Suddenly I was out of my body, feeling totally peaceful and comfortable, watching this boy on the bed dying. It never occurred to me, *How can I see this?*

"I was watching this boy die and feeling glad I was no longer the boy. *Even without a brain, this is wonderful. If this is what dead is, I want to be dead.* I knew my parents would be sad, but I didn't want to go back.

"Suddenly it felt like an angel did a Heimlich maneuver on me. Then the boy on the bed vomited, dislodged the pieces, and started breathing. I felt myself sucked back into my body as if through a vacuum cleaner. I thought, *Someone had a schedule and I wasn't supposed to die. I wanted to die, so who's making these decisions for me?* I yelled out, '*WHO DID THAT?*' But no one was there.

"I was mad as hell to come back and leave the freedom I felt during my NDE. I wanted to be out of my body because of the choking and spasms. I can't put into words how painful that was. There was no pain during my NDE, no problems. I was free! *This is neat—who wants to be in a body?*

"I realized I wasn't the body, I was Spirit. It was wonderful being out there looking around. My mother would have found me dead, but I preferred death over life."

He never discussed this NDE with his mother. "My mother was too upset so I couldn't tell her how wonderful it was."

Bernie didn't experience the Light like many NDErs. "I was going toward the Light but it was as if someone pulled me back, so I never got far enough to see it. I had no sense of time. It might have been two minutes or ten, but it happened very quickly. When my body took a breath, it pulled me back in."

Ultimately, he used the experience to improve his life as well as the lives of others. "When I was seven years old, I said I wanted to become a doctor. I liked people and I liked to fix things. I thought I would take care of people and fix them, but later I realized I can't fix everyone."

Bernie believes his NDE helped him become a better doctor. "My NDE always made a difference in my life. I became a doctor to save lives, then got interested in death and dying, and started support groups for people with cancer and other life-threatening illnesses. I wanted people to know that death is not the worst outcome. If you want to keep living, great. If you get tired, I'll assist you to find comfort. It's okay to let go and die. Because I'm not afraid, I can help people with their fears about death and dying. I can be there with them and not have to cover up or deny things. I can just be present for them."

Although he can't fix everyone, Bernie understands that he can always help. "I can't remove their grief and the pain of being separated from their family and children. Every life is a candle that burns for a certain period and then the flame goes out. It's important for people to know that God is not punishing them because someone they love has died."

Bernie likes to hear about his patients' experiences when he suspects they have left their bodies. "When I asked patients if they had an NDE, they often denied it until they read about it in books and realized it's okay to talk about it. They were afraid people would think they were nuts, or they would try to attribute it to a mechanical problem with the brain."

As patients felt more comfortable with the subject of NDEs, they started sharing their stories with Bernie, although many physicians have a hard time accepting the concept.

"Why not say *I can't explain it* instead of denying it's possible?" Bernie asks. "I think a lot of the rejection of NDEs has to do with how we're trained as physicians. In medical school, we didn't

There Is More . . .

learn about consciousness, only the body. For me, working with Elisabeth Kübler-Ross on the subject of Spirits and a whole host of other things assisted me to understand more.

"Knowing about NDEs, the spirit realm, dying, and death has also saved lives. I remember operating on a man and his heart stopped. They pronounced him dead, and one of the medical people turned to leave the operating room. Before knowing about Elisabeth's work, I wouldn't have thought of it, but I knew his Spirit was still around. So I called out the patient's name and yelled, 'It's not your time yet, so come on back!' The man started breathing. One of the medical staff looked at me and said, 'From now on, I'm going to work with you.' Another one felt disturbed and denied the event.

"Ultimately, the only thing you can control is your thoughts. When you quiet your mind, the truth becomes apparent and you realize your connection. We all come from the same thing and we don't need an introduction to that intelligent, loving conscious energy I call God. I can operate on people and they will heal—it's built into us. How amazing is that?

"If I love my life, my body will do everything possible to keep me alive.

"When our seven-year-old son had a bone tumor, he told me, 'You're handling this poorly, you're worrying about next year.' He was right. Life is about enjoying the moment."

Dr. Bernie Siegel is known internationally for his compassion, wisdom, and love that shine brightly in his books, seminars, and presence. Since 1978, he has talked about patient empowerment and the choice to live fully and die in peace. Bernie has counseled innumerable people whose lives have been threatened by illness.

Today, Bernie writes, runs support groups, lectures, and spends as much time as possible with his wife, Bobbie, and their family. He enjoys caring for their pets and doing what makes him happy. He says, "There is no spare time; there is only my life time."

Among the many books Bernie has written are *Love, Medicine and Miracles: Lessons Learned about Self-Healing from a Surgeon's Experience with Exceptional Patients*; *365 Prescriptions for the Soul: Daily Messages of Inspiration, Hope, and Love*; *101 Exercises for the Soul: Divine Workout Plan for Body, Mind, and Spirit*.

Dr. Bernie Siegel and Jennifer Sander co-wrote *Faith, Hope and Healing: Inspiring Lessons Learned from People Living with Cancer*.

To learn more about Dr. Siegel, go to BernieSiegelMD.com.

I first met Bernie in the mid-1980s when we spoke at the same AIDS conferences (AIDS Medicine and Miracles). He is a man who walks his truth, and one of the most amazing men I know— an individual filled with Life, Light, and Love! As a medical doctor recognized throughout the world, his message and wisdom is received by millions with open hearts.

When Bernie was choking to death as a child, he saw his physical body dying. He felt his Spirit lift and hover over his body, and he felt freedom and love, not fear.

His experience shows us that we are not our bodies. Our bodies are vehicles for traveling this planet, and they carry our spirits.

There Is More . . .

When we release our physical bodies, we become whole in a way we've never experienced on this Earth plane, free from pain, constriction, and limits. We become whole with Love—something for us all to remember and embrace as we age and draw closer to that time of transition.

While in the physical form, touch is a powerful healing technique. When Bernie's grandmother used massage to help him adjust after his difficult birth, she used one of the most ancient and available methods of healing. Don't underestimate the power of touch.

When someone is in need, perhaps stressed, ill, or even dying, it is important to nurture that person to the best of our ability. When you are wrapped up in your own emotions you are not available for the other person.

Bernie's son knew this, and he reminded his dad that the present moment is what matters the most. Being present is the best gift we can give, to ourselves and to others. Sometimes it means being a physical part of the healing or transition, other times it may require we step back and allow the person to heal in a quiet space. Everyone is different and their needs may change with time.

✧
Tessa
Overwhelmed

A wise six year old, Tessa has short brown shoulder-length hair and hazel eyes.

She attends first grade at a Waldorf School. Tessa loves her school because they don't use plastic, only wood and natural materials. She likes to draw, color, and make crafts. She enjoys sketching people, horses, and princesses. "We don't use pointed crayons at my school; we use block crayons instead," she's proud to say. I also like the teachers because they are nice to everyone.

"At home, I love to play with my dolls. I also like animals, science and origami." She smiled, "I have origami paper in every color of the rainbow."

When I asked Tessa to share her near-death experience, here's what she said.

"About two years ago I was in bed when an angel appeared. She looked solid. She wore a long pink dress and a rose in her hair. Her hair is brown like mine, but my angel wears braids. I feel real special when she's around me."

Tessa said her angel comforts her when she's sad and plays with her. "My angel rocks me in her arms and plays dolls with me. We like to play outside. It's snowing right now and I've played outside twice today with my angel. We made snowballs, a snowman, and snow angels."

There Is More . . .

Tessa told me many angels come to her but this one is special. "My angel tells me stories about animals, science, and the future.

"She tells me how the animals migrate. My favorite animal is the cheetah because it's the fastest. She also teaches me how to communicate with animals, plants, and trees."

When Tessa told me that, it warmed my heart. It reminded me of when Laura, my angel, taught me how to do the same things.

"She also teaches me how to use numbers, tells me stories about the future with volcano eruptions, Earth changes, and tornadoes."

"Tessa, does that scare you?"

"No, because my angel told me not to be afraid, but be aware of these things and how they happen."

Tessa seemed eager to share. "She taught me how to behave. She told me anger doesn't help anything, and if I get mad, I should walk away from other people."

"Do you share your teachings and stories with your mommy and auntie?" I asked.

"No, the angels don't want me to tell the grown ups because adults have lost sight of being a child."

"Tessa, is your special angel with you now?"

With a big smile on her face and a sparkle in her eye, she said, "Yes, she's sitting next to me. She's with me a lot."

"Tessa, how do you hear your angel?"

"Usually, when I watch her or look at her, she uses hand signals. Then I listen and imagine what is being said."

"Do you ever ask your angel questions?"

"No, I just listen to her stories and learn from her. I'm happy about the stories because I like to learn stuff."

"Would you ask your angel if you can ask her a question for me?"

She immediately asked out loud, "Angel, can I ask a question?" Then Tessa nodded and her eyes opened wide. "She said you can ask her a question."

"When I was young, I had a special angel named Laura. Will you ask your angel what her name is?"

"What's your name?" Tessa giggled. "She said her name is Alice."

I couldn't help but smile. "Please thank Alice for telling you her name and for being your angel."

Tessa did so out loud, then told me, "It's nice knowing her name. Thank you for helping me find out what it is."

"You're welcome. Now you can call her anytime you want by her name. My angel, Laura, wore a long pink gown like your angel, and she spoke to me. We used to play dolls. Laura taught me how to communicate with plants, animals, trees, flowers, and other angels."

Excited, Tessa blurted, "Really?"

"Really. Would you ask Alice if she knows my angel, Laura?"

There Is More . . .

"Alice, do you know Sharon's angel named Laura?" Even more excited, Tessa's eyes flashed. "Yes, they know each other. They play and do things together!"

My heart filled with joy and excitement. "Tessa, do your mommy and auntie believe in angels?"

She shrugged. "They say angels are nice, kind, and giving. They have angels, too, but can't see them. I just know they have them. Alice said she will send big angels to them."

"Tessa, will you please ask Alice what you were doing when you first saw her?"

"I know what I was doing. I was sitting on my bed playing with my toys and dolls. I have a favorite doll named Barbara."

"Were you happy when your angel came to you the first time?"

"Oh yes, very happy."

"Will you ask Alice why she came to you?"

"Alice, why did you come to me?" Tessa pauses for a moment, then tells me, "Alice said she's my angel and I never have to worry about something scary happening to me again. I feel safe, happy, and loved when she's around me."

I knew how fragile Tessa was, so I didn't pursue the question. But I did glean that sometime in her past, Tessa experienced something so frightening she doesn't recall the circumstances. Yet her angel, Alice, protected her and became her friend.

"Is there anything else Alice has taught you?"

Tessa said, "She introduced me to Jesus and God. I talk to them like I do to the angels. I see them. Jesus just gave Alice a white flower with a center that looks like yellow rose petals. It's a gift for being kind and loving to me."

Tears filled my eyes. "Tessa, will you please thank Alice for loving and protecting you?"

"Alice, thank you for loving and protecting me." Then Tessa turned back to me. "She said you're welcome. She loves me."

I smiled and nodded. "Tessa, is there anything else you see, hear, or feel that most children your age don't?"

"I see patterns and designs around people, plants, and trees. They're usually pretty designs. Sometimes I see mixed-up colors that aren't so pretty."

"Can you tell me when you've seen the mixed-up colors that aren't so pretty?"

"Once, two bullies at school punched me and hurt other kids. I could see black and gray around them and it's ugly. I know red, pink, purple, green, and gold are good colors, but black and gray mean something is wrong or bad."

Suddenly excited, she added, "Gold is very special."

She paused, then continued. "When I hear loud sounds, I get stressed out and scared. A few days ago at school, the teachers took us to a science event. There, they shot water that sounded like fireworks—and that scared me. I asked my teacher if we could go back to our classroom. Alice stayed close to me and put her arm around me."

There Is More . . .

My heart opened up so wide. "Tessa, you're blessed to have Alice and your angel friends."

"Yeah, I know." Tessa continued, "I had two dogs and one died. I have two cats and a couple of fish and two chickens and a mouse. Alice was sad when my dog Gracie died, and so was I."

"I'll bet Alice comforted you."

"Yeah."

"Will you give Alice a big kiss for letting me know about her?"

Tessa kissed the air next to her.

"What's Alice doing now?"

"Her wings are expanding and her red heart is expanding and slowing. There's White Light coming from her heart. Her face is pale with blue eyes but there's gold around her face. She liked the kiss."

"What are you and Alice going to do the rest of the day?"

"Play in the meadow and snow."

"Can you ask Alice if your mommy and auntie can join you two?"

She asked, then replied, "Yes, they can. Alice is going to send two big angels to play with mommy and auntie."

When Tessa grows up, she wants to be a mommy and an actress.

What a blessing to be able to experience the love this little girl feels for life and the world! Meeting Tessa reaffirms my belief in pure love, innocence, beauty, and grace.

Often children don't lose their abilities to see and hear from the spirit realm until parents, teachers, or other children tell them they're make-believe friends. It's important for parents to realize children do have the gift of seeing and hearing the spirit realm, and as adults we can learn from them by asking questions about what they see, hear, and sense.

If you have young children, ask your child to ask their Spirit friends questions about the other realm and lessons we can learn.

As people go through the dying process, the abilities to see and hear the spirit realm often reawaken. If your loved ones express sensing a departed loved one or claim to see the Light of God or love, believe them. Ask questions. Often they are sensing the "other" realm, and the information they share may help you in your own life.

Angel stories are present on every continent and in most religions. We've all heard stories of superhuman strength, a silent stranger who helps in the exact time of need, or an animal that shows up right when someone needs extra love.

Everyone has angels and Spirits eager to assist them in their journeys, but they're not allowed to interfere with your life. You must call upon them before they can help. When you do, know there's an infinite supply of wisdom in the spiritual realm.

Adolescent Experiences

Near-Death Experiences (NDEs)

Distressing Near-Death Experiences (dNDEs)

Out-of-Body Experiences (OBEs)

Spiritual Transformative Experiences (STEs)

Dominique
Repeatedly Abused

Dominique grew up in Europe. Her parents divorced when she was twelve, and because she had experienced abuse as a child, she thought about suicide often. "I became a depressed, troubled teenager, often in therapy because of suicidal thoughts, and I've wanted to die since I was twelve years old."

From age twelve to seventeen, Dominique was promiscuous. Kids beat her up at school and one boy tried to rape her at age fourteen, but she got away. She became so depressed, she stopped eating. Her mother sent Dominique away to a boarding school. "I know my mother meant well, but it was still very hard for me to be sent away. There wasn't anyone there for me. In boarding school, I attempted suicide—I stood at the edge of a balcony, ready to jump and end my pain, when a teacher pulled me back and saved me. I then took an overdose of painkillers, but I threw them up. It got the school's attention and that's when my therapy started." A therapist from outside the school visited Dominique once a week, but it didn't help.

"At seventeen, I was looking for someone to help me get my life back on track. A social worker invited me over to his apartment to fill out paperwork, and while I was there he drugged, beat, and raped me, and then sexually assaulted me with a knife. I was in a coma for two days from the drugs. Afterward, I could no longer handle my pain. I went to therapy for years, but again nothing helped."

She was so vulnerable at the time of the assault. "I was reaching out for help, and his attack was brutal. During the rape, he kept telling me that I was a whore, so that got stuck in my head." She blamed herself for trusting him enough to enter his apartment, and questioned why a social worker would hurt people. She's working to find peace now, but a small part of her still feels at fault for trusting him.

The recurring abuse confused Dominique and she felt she shouldn't be alive. "I didn't feel worthy to be carried by this Earth. I didn't feel loved by life." Attempting to be undesirable to men, she shaved her head, wore baggy boy's clothes to hide her body, and hung around with punks on the street. Her parents didn't know how to help, but they never gave up on her.

Dominique had her NDE at the age of seventeen. "I was so depressed and a guy from school offered me some drugs, a powder, to lift my spirits. I sniffed a long line up my nose. It was painful and I felt like I was going to die."

She felt as if she committed a crime against herself. She went to class and within ten minutes, the teacher sent her home because she looked sick.

As she headed toward the train, she collapsed on a stone bench and the last thing she saw was the nearby river and ducks. "Everything went black, then it was like waking up from a nightmare. I felt completely alive—on fire like I had never felt before. I floated outside my body, above myself. It happened in the blink of an eye. I became more alert than ever before, then I panicked because I didn't understand what was happening. I didn't understand I'd died.

"I'm not sitting, I'm not standing, and I'm not lying down. How am I existing? A feeling of enormous regret came over me like I had violated my life and punished myself, and I was extremely angry at myself."

Dominique

Dominique felt terrified. "There was no going back. I had gone over the edge and couldn't return to my body."

She floated to the tops of the trees, looked over the entire city, and knew what time it was—2:00 p.m. Dominique thought of her mom, father, and siblings, and realized she was separated from them and could never see them again. "This was a sadness I had never felt before, unbearable. It was like everyone died at the same time because I left. I didn't want to let go of my mother—I loved her so very much."

She felt a change of heart. "I was full of regret and repentance. *Give me one more chance. Let me live again and change my life.* I realized I felt love and I wanted to live."

Dominique saw the paramedics arrive and noticed them moving something around on the stone bench, but she didn't realize it was her body.

They moved quickly. They called her middle name, as it was listed on her ID as her first. She understood they were trying to call her back to her body.

"*I don't want to die!* I screamed into their faces, but they couldn't see me. I felt invisible and it was horrible. Then everything went black and I was sucked back inside my body after they loaded it into the ambulance."

She had felt complete freedom outside her body. Now, strapped down to the gurney, she felt tight, squeezed back into a tiny, limiting body.

They called Dominique a junkie, but even though she told them she wasn't a drug addict, they gave her an injection to counteract heroin and drove her to the police station. She told them she needed to go to the hospital, but they didn't care. "The way I was treated was completely degrading and dehumanizing. The police took my photo and carried away all my belongings. I kept telling them I needed to see a doctor and they insisted that all I needed was to walk up and down the hall to get my circulation going.

"I need to sit down, right now!" she shouted, but they wouldn't let her. "I felt dizzy, felt all my strength leave my body. I felt awful . . . I was dying and I knew it. Then I fell over.

"I didn't feel myself hit the floor. I was out of my body again, and it wasn't frightening this time. They took my body to an area in the police station where they attempted CPR. An ambulance came and they gave me electric shocks. I floated in the room and noticed a cross on the wall. I wasn't scared this time. I hadn't done this; it was done *to* me. I had died before so I wasn't scared.

"Everything went black and they revived me. I was in the emergency room and unconscious when I went back into my body.

"They found the residue from what I sniffed up my nose—it was rat poison. They said I was lucky to be alive."

Dominique was in the hospital only three hours before they turned her back over to the police. She had grown up in a different country, had a strong accent, and didn't have her passport with her to prove she was legally in the country she now lived in. The police told her they were going to deport her.

"They took me to a deportation center that night. I insisted they needed to contact my mother, to confirm that I was a legal citizen. They didn't listen, but handcuffed me to a prostitute and drove me toward the border. I kept screaming, 'Please call my mother. I am legally in the country!' They told me they had spoken to her and she said that because I had taken drugs, she never wanted to see me again and they should take me away. I was devastated. However, it fortunately turned out to be a lie.

"When we arrived at the border and the police were ready to let me out into nowhere, they got a call from my mother confirming my legal resident status. They brought me back and my mother met me at the police station. I embraced her like never before. I didn't want to let go of her.

"Now, I no longer want to die. My NDE changed my life. Before, I didn't know what death was like. I used to think that once you die, it's over. Now I realize that after death, you're still alive, you still feel and think. I needed to work through my issues in this life, and only let go of life once *I'm* ready to make my transition."

Dominique is afraid of the dark. "I'm thirty-three years old now, and the darkness reminds me of my first NDE, so I sleep with the lights on. My husband doesn't like it, but now he's used to it.

"Since my NDE, I'm more sensitive to sound and my heart races when something startles me. I'm definitely jumpy. When I get sick and throw up, it reminds me of the rat poison and part of me relives this difficult memory every time."

She mentioned she was surprised she didn't see the Light and tunnel or hear the voices everyone talks about. "I thought I must have been a bad person because I never saw any of that. What I learned from the International Association of Near-Death Studies or IANDS is that I had a *distressing* near-death experience, or a dNDE."

In 1993 when Dominique had this experience, there was little research about dNDEs. When she shared her story, people told her God had rejected her and that she was a bad person because she didn't see the Light. "'*You went to Hell*,' they told me. So I stopped sharing my story."

In 1998, Dominique had a Spiritually Transformative Experience (STE). "One day Mormon missionaries knocked on my door and convinced me to pray and ask God if he was there. I told God I didn't feel loved. After six weeks of wrestling with myself and kneeling down to pray, one night something came over me and I felt scared. I jumped into bed and pulled the sheets and blankets over my head. Suddenly it was as if a curtain ripped open and I saw my life flash before my eyes. I saw everything I was ashamed of. Then I felt forgiveness and a new start. I hadn't recognized the Light of God before, but on that night, it came to me and embraced me. I felt like I was on fire with complete love. I realized I could feel love and have a purpose."

She called the Light "God," however, she felt that the Light was flexible about the words. "The Mormon Church got me to pray, but I am still Jewish. Through my prayers, love came to me. I asked for love and I was ready to feel it. Love is the most powerful force—it goes beyond everything and it's unconditional and available for everyone."

Ever since her STE, Dominique has felt happy and lives her life with purpose. "I made contact with God and it transformed me. I told my mother I needed to move out and completely start over—new friends, clothes, music, and an entirely new lifestyle. I wanted to become a different person and do what is right.

"God's love and forgiveness was all powerful and all consuming, and it made me recognize what we are. I love people now. I see how special people are. In the Light, I forgave myself in love, and that Light and love has stayed with me."

In 2005, she attended a meeting of the Los Angeles International Association of Near-Death Studies (IANDS). The people there understood her dNDE and what happened to her. "That's when I began to heal."

More information on dNDEs has become available since her experience in 1993, and Dominique doesn't get judged harshly anymore. Still, she's sometimes apprehensive about sharing her story because it was a scary time. "I believe my *next* death will be beautiful," she said. "I've prepared myself and I meditate often. I'm at peace in my heart and can live with my first two death experiences now."

As we neared the end of our interview, Dominique's energy felt much lighter, her face looked brighter and happier, and she giggled like a child.

"My two experiences changed my life because I'm more understanding of people now. I'm a lot more forgiving of others and myself. I love people more, see the value of life, and understand joy. During my NDE, I was consumed by grief with nothing to fall back on. Now I have a greater appreciation for my body—it's temporary and it's a gift.

"I do believe I have something to say and I incorporate it in my work. I share my message of love, understanding, and compassion, and that's my purpose in life. Even though I rejected myself for so long, I learned to accept myself and others."

Dominique believes many religious institutions use fear to scare people. She joined a church because others said she was a bad person and that's why she didn't see the Light. "Sometimes religions like to control people. I wasn't in Hell, yet people said I was. They told me I needed to get baptized to go to Heaven next time and avoid another 'Hell' experience. It's a trick.

"I believe in the principle of Oneness as my religion. NDErs long for spirituality and it's important people don't abuse that."

Dominique works in the entertainment arts today. She weaves her story throughout everything she creates. "There's always something I learned in my NDE that pops up in my work."

Dominique got married in 2000. Her husband is loving, supportive, and understanding of her experiences. The greatest blessing of her life, however, is their child. "The day my son was born, I knew why I survived."

My heart felt heavy as Dominique started to share her experiences. However, I know that because of her challenges, she has become a brighter light and is able to connect to people at a deeper level with compassion and understanding.

Like so many adolescents around the world, Dominique felt lost, alone, misunderstood, grief-stricken, and depressed. She no longer felt connected to her parents and had to find a way to survive. She encountered rape and betrayal from a counselor, betrayed herself by not listening to her inner voice that warned her not to go to the counselor's apartment alone, then was betrayed by the police who were supposed to protect her.

Through it all, the message was to love herself, and she finally understood this once she reconnected with herself, her mother, and God.

You, too, are an expression of God. Care for your Spirit. Cherish and nurture your Self with positive thoughts, feelings, and self-care. Treat yourself as if you were a young child, which you still are inside. We all deserve loving kindness, no matter who we are in society.

Dominique's intuition told her she was dying and needed to go to the hospital, yet initially the police disregarded her request. All of us have intuition, an inner knowing. It might start out like a twinge, a pain, or a small voice within, but each of us has the ability to be guided by our intuition. We just need to trust it.

Test it. It's the only way to know for certain. Once you attain trust in your Self and your intuition, it can save your life. You have the connection—now turn on the Light.

Colter Rios
Paralyzed from a Football Injury

I saw fear in Colter's dark eyes as he described the scene surrounding his accident and out-of-body experience (OBE). He was nervous about talking to me, but the uneasiness went beyond our interview. He had feared death on that football field.

Colter's life before his out-of-body experience was filled with high school baseball, football, schoolwork, activities, and family. As a star athlete, he was used to championship games, high pressure to win, and dealing with the normal bruises of athletics.

On October 19, 2007, one of Colter's high school football games got rougher than normal and he landed on his neck. "Everything stopped. It felt like I was floating side to side up into the air and everything got silent. The crowd noise was gone and everything around me went quiet." He saw himself on the ground with his eyes still open, but he continued to rise, away from his body. He remembers asking God, "Please, don't take me."

Then he immediately dropped back into his body, experiencing the same lurching stomach as when he rode on an airplane at take-off and the G-forces pulled on his body.

"I didn't want to go, I wanted to stay. I felt it was too early—it wasn't my time to die."

Colter, paralyzed, was rushed to the hospital on a backboard. Miraculously, in about a week, he could walk again, but he couldn't move his hands for a week and a half. After days of therapy, medications, and tests, his doctors told him to grab a

There Is More . . .

cup. When he couldn't, a doctor told his parents he would never use his hands normally again and would need help feeding himself.

With a smile, Colter said, "I knew they were wrong."

"My family gave me the drive to come home and be normal again. I saw the softer side of my dad and the stronger side of my mom. They were amazing."

Other people had a hand in his speedy recovery. In the hospital, he had a roommate for a day who told him, "No matter what you do, think about the present. Live for the moment, work for the moment. If you think about a year from now, a month from now, even a week from now, you'll drive yourself crazy. Just work for the moment."

Ever since Colter heard that advice, that's what he's done—it served him well.

Colter looks at life differently now. He appreciates his family and being able to walk and feed himself. Little things make him happy, like waking up at home, spending time with friends, and living in the moment.

Before he went into surgery, he said it was scary, but he knew he would be okay, even though it made no sense for a spinal cord injury patient to have everything normal again. His faith was very strong.

As Colter was prepped for surgery, he remembers looking up at his doctor. "The doctor's eyes were really blue. I'd never seen eyes that blue, and then the doctor's face turned into my grandfather's face. That's when I knew everything would be all right." His grandfather had passed away, but Colter knew his grandfather was still looking after him, and everything would turn out fine.

After surgery, Colter's family came into his recovery room, and his sister told him she had made homecoming court. "She told me she wished I'd walk her out onto the field for the event." He told his sister he'd do it. Only two weeks away, it was unlikely he'd be out of the hospital, let alone walking. Yet Colter was determined to keep his promise.

"The day I was released from the hospital," Colter said with a sweet smile, "was the day I walked her out for homecoming. That was the best feeling ever. Everyone was standing up. I've never had so many people cheer for me. I've played in huge games, championships, and I've never heard the crowd so loud. It was the best welcome back I could have had."

Since this experience, Colter returned to school and has played some sports. After his accident, he had heightened senses, such as touch, smell and sight. "Touch is intensified, even now. Getting hit in sports hurts much more than before. I used to ignore it. Now it bothers me. It's hard for other people to understand that, especially coaches.

"I took a lot for granted before. I appreciate natural talent so much more now. I think a lot of kids my age take walking, their family, and activities for granted. At any moment, your life can be taken away.

"I used to spend all my time looking down the road, what I'd be doing in the future, planning for college and beyond. Now, I live for the present, and I have a stronger connection to everyone."

There Is More . . .

Colter graduated from high school in 2010 with honors. He looks forward to a rich college experience at Redlands University in Redlands, California, where he plans to specialize in environmental studies. Colter will also be on the baseball team, either at second base or center field. He continues to value the time he spends with his family and friends.

Getting to know Colter was a joy. I can see him becoming a mentor and motivational speaker. Through his injury, he was blessed to reclaim his life and start living it more fully with gratitude.

As an active high school student and athlete, Colter was popular and, like many kids his age, took life for granted. His spinal injury made him realize that little things such as eating, walking, playing sports, waking up in his home, and being available to his family are precious. He no longer takes these things for granted.

There's a strong Spirit within Colter, an inner knowing that everything would be okay, even when doctors told him he wouldn't fully recover. His experience shows how the power of belief can see us through difficult situations and can help create miracles.

As with the Law of Attraction, we can expect the best and direct thoughts, words, emotions, and actions toward the outcome of our heart's desires. We can manifest almost anything through faith and hard work.

Colter proved that to himself and many others, and his Light will continue to shine. He has a bright future.

✧ ✧ ✧

Adult Experiences

Near-Death Experiences (NDEs)

Out-of-Body Experiences (OBEs)

Spiritual Transformative Experiences (STEs)

Sharon Lund, DD
Suicide Attempts and AIDS Complications

For the first thirty-five years of my life, I had low self-esteem. From the outside, I looked and acted as if I had it all together, but on the inside, I was dying. I was killing myself, beating myself up with words, thoughts, and actions.

Nine years of being raped as a child, never feeling like I fitted in at school, and certain destructive and abusive relationships had ripped me apart. I felt worthless, powerless, and undeserving. I attempted to cover up my feelings by becoming a people-pleaser, caregiver, and rescuer.

My low self-esteem led me to attract several destructive relationships—one physically abusive and the other emotionally and verbally abusive. Because of the years of abuse as a child and adult, I believed the only way to end my suffering and pain was to kill myself.

In 1984, I attempted suicide twice, first with a bottle of pills. I felt angry because I couldn't keep them down. A few days later, I leaned against the bathtub and held a shiny razor to my left wrist. Out loud, I said my final prayer, "God, please forgive me for what I'm about to do. I have to end my pain and suffering. If there's anything I need to know before I kill myself, let me know right now."

Immediately, the entire bathroom filled with beautiful, loving, warm, bright Light. A sense of peace and love permeated my entire Being. I heard the voice of Infinite Spirit say, *My Child, it's not your time to die. Get yourself into the hospital and when*

There Is More . . .

you return, you will become a healer, teach around the world, and write books.

None of that made sense to me, but I knew I had received my life purpose. I felt grateful Infinite Spirit showed me a better way than committing suicide. I checked myself into the hospital for anorexia and suicide attempts, and I stayed for three months. While in the hospital, part of my healing was to call my parents and tell them about my grandfather raping me from age three to twelve (it ended when he died).

I'll never forget the rage I heard in my dad's voice as he told me, "If my father were alive today, I would kill him." From that moment on, my relationship with my dad changed forever. I deeply felt in my heart that if he had known, he would have protected me.

My mom's response was different. I was aware that both my parents had been severely abused as they were growing up. Her response to the abuse I suffered from my grandfather was, "At least you didn't have it as bad as I did when I was growing up." She never shared the details of her abuse.

While in the hospital I felt blessed because I became aware of two of my Spirit guides. Vira Cocha (Wiracocha known in Peru) spoke with immense compassion and love. When I felt Vira Cocha's presence and heard his voice, a deep sense of inner peace filled my soul, and my heart relaxed into a state of magnificent love.

Also during that time, an old Japanese man—about four-foot-nine with a long white beard and tall staff—stood before my bed and said he had come to teach me about Eastern healing therapies and philosophies. His name is Semitar.

When I left the hospital, I searched for the truth and found it had been within me all along—just like Dorothy and the ruby slippers.

After connecting with the Light of Infinite Spirit, I had healing and psychic abilities I never had before. I could scan a person's body and see what was wrong, then do energy work to clear the problem. I saw events in the future, and much of what I saw I didn't like. I heard in meditation how to work with this ability so I could assist the person or situation before the event took place. After a few years, I blocked out seeing future events, but my senses were still heightened, and colors and sounds were profound.

In early 1986, I began volunteering in the cancer and HIV/AIDS communities, doing healings and teaching processes, body dialogue, affirmations, visualizations, meditations, muscle testing, and other things I learned after being in the Light. I felt secure with my life, loved the person I had become, and was living my life purpose.

In December 1986, while watching Dan Rather's AIDS special on network television, *AIDS Hits Home*, I recognized my ex-husband, Bill, and heard him announce to the audience he was infected with AIDS and had led a secret bisexual life. I called Bill and he denied it was him on the show (his face had been blocked), but in meditation I heard that it *was* him and knew I needed to be tested. My tests came back positive for HIV. Bill called me a few years later, just before he died, and admitted that when he married me in 1983, he was living a secret bisexual lifestyle and knew he was infected.

After my HIV diagnosis (known at the time as ARC—AIDS Related Complex), the doctor said I would die within six months if I didn't take AZT, a new medication. I asked in meditation if taking the drug was for my highest good and I heard, *"No! Do not take AZT."*

I figured I would die within six months, so I got my final affairs together and asked my parents if they would raise my daughter, Jeaneen, when I died. They agreed.

Then I heard in meditation, *Why have you made your doctor God? Why have you bought into his death sentence? He doesn't know how or when you're going to die.*

That was an immediate wake-up call. I had bought into my doctor's death sentence! I fired my doctor and found one who believed in healing through integrating mind, body, and spirit.

For many years, I only had three T-cells. I named them Hope, Love, and Laughter and gave them the power and permission to assist me to heal. I allowed the virus to empower me. I stopped taking life for granted, took better care of my health, and applied the mind-body-spirit healing techniques I had been teaching. I became one of the first women in Southern California to go public about being infected. Before long, I traveled throughout the United States and Canada, Russia, Europe, and Japan, sharing my wisdom, life experiences, and blessings that came from each and every challenge. I appeared on *The Oprah Winfrey Show, 48 Hours, Eye on America, CNN,* and was featured in *"O" The Oprah Magazine, Shape, Women's World,* and the front page of the *Los Angeles Times.*

Finally, after nine years of working and volunteering, I burned out. I heard in meditation, *My Child, you need to move to the red rocks for healing.* In 1995, I was Divinely guided to my new home in a community outside of St. George, Utah, called Kayenta. The moment I saw Kayenta, I cried. I knew I had found my home. The magnificent red rocks surrounded the quiet environment, offering peace of mind.

However, in 1996, I danced with death again due to AIDS complications: PCP (pneumocystis carinii pneumonia) and MAC (mycobacterium avium complex).

I was so angry at Infinite Spirit and my guides that I turned my back on them. I stopped praying and meditating. My mom and daughter noticed how I was giving up on life and kept insisting I reconnect with the God within me. I spent over a month in fierce anger until, finally, I surrendered and prayed. *God, why have you brought me here and left me this way? You guided me to the red rocks for healing and now I'm dying.*

Then I heard: *My Child, I never left you. I have always been with you and always will be. It was you who turned your back on me.*

I broke down and cried. Then I immediately reconnected with Infinite Spirit and my spirit guides, Vira Cocha and Semitar.

For a year and a half, I spent more time in the hospital than out. In March 1997, my daughter Jeaneen, my parents, and my sister Joyce were told I probably wouldn't make it through the weekend.

This is how I describe my life from 1996-97 while I was in the hospital:

My life force feels weak and dim. I lie helpless in a cold, sterile hospital bed, hooked up to IVs for treatments and transfusions. Implanted in my chest is a Hickman catheter, a special device for feedings, and deep within me, a catheter is embedded, its tubing ending in a bag to collect my urine. As I gasp for air, a nurse hooks me up to oxygen. Each breath of life becomes more precious and difficult.

I lost my independence. I cannot care for myself. I buzz the nurse to adjust my skeletal body, to ease my pain.

A handful of pills, one more shot, one more IV, a familiar face exploring my body. My sheets, gown, pillow, and entire body feel drenched with sweat. My fevers register over 103 degrees, then chills run through me, cold as ice. Lying in bed, I suddenly start to shake and clench my fists, thinking it is an earthquake. But it's not, it's me, shivering. When will it end? The tubes, the suffering, the emotions and confusion. Is death knocking at my door?

Nothing stays in my body. The stench of vomit and diarrhea envelops and permeates my surroundings. Day in and day out, endlessly the same. Am I living? I fear not. I feel no vitality or quality of life. I would much rather die than live in my condition. I suffer and so does my family. I feel my life slipping away.

I'm not ready to die yet. My heart and soul ache for my daughter, Jeaneen. I must embrace her one more time.

March 1997:

I see Jeaneen walk into the doorway of my hospital room. She stands by the door and looks at me as though I were a stranger. As I catch a glimpse of her, the room seems to light up and a surge of energy sweeps over me. A sense of calm fills my soul as my heart swells at the sight of my beloved daughter. Yet it frightens me that she continues to stand in the doorway. As she stares at me, I realize my thin, pasty body must be a pathetic sight.

Then she bursts into tears, dashes toward me, bends over the hospital bed, and slides her arms around me. Tears stream down our cheeks as we embrace. I feel my body shake with excitement.

"Mommy! I love you!"

I manage to gather enough strength to say, "I love you."

After regaining what little composure I can muster, she asks, "Mom, can I stay here with you all night?"

My eyes must gleam as I nod, "Yes!"

She lowers the bed safety rail, sits next to me, and holds my hand. Softly she places her hands on my face, looks into my eyes, and tells me how much she loves and misses me. Tears roll down our faces. Jeaneen smiles as she wipes my runny nose with a tissue and then lightly rubs away my teardrops—and hers.

"Oh, Mommy, I want to make you well. I want to do things together again. I want to bring you home and take care of you."

I want to smile at her, but it feels as if a knife slices me open and rips out my insides. Jeaneen asks, "Mom, can I crawl into bed with you and hold you in my arms? I'll try not to move or hurt you." I welcome her to join me. Jeaneen climbs into bed next to me and holds me, kisses me, spoons with me. The warmth of her body next to mine and her hand and arm on my chest make me feel safe and loved. I feel my shoulder get moist from her tears. Jeaneen knows my intense love for her by my actions, words, support, guidance, and freedom to express herself, which I gave her throughout her life. A loving look, a gentle caress, our special kiss, holding hands as we did so often. These simple things bring me comfort.

I fall asleep in Jeaneen's arms. Throughout the night, we don't rest much. In the morning when breakfast arrives for Jeaneen, I can tell she's exhausted. After she eats, she asks, "Mom, if you don't mind, I'd like to drive back to your house and take a shower. I'll be right back. Do you want anything from home?"

I smile and say, "Just you." I watch as she slowly walks out into the corridor.

My body trembles and I become weaker. I'm awake and alone— or thought I was alone! All of a sudden, my Spirit lifts and hovers over my physical body lying in the bed below. I immediately feel healed, more alive and free than ever before. Love and inner peace cascade from within me.

After my Spirit floats over my body for a short time, two Spirit Beings, one male and one female, appear before me. They wear long white gowns. They look physical, yet I can see through them, just like Laura and my other spirit guides who have been with me for so many years. The Spirit Beings reach out and take my hand. Telepathically, they tell me they want to show me a review of my life.

In an instant, I'm looking down at different scenes and events in my lifetime with numerous people and situations from around the world. As I witness the scenes, telepathically the Spirit Beings say, "Look at the difference you made in their lives." After I see numerous events and people I had forgotten, and the difference I made in so many lives, the Spirit Beings take me away.

I feel myself upright and horizontally move into and through a bright tunnel of Light. I notice gray figures like people on the outside of the tunnel, attempting to reach out and touch me. Swiftly I pass unfamiliar faces looking at me. I want to cry out, "Where are my brothers, Tommy and Raymond? Where are my friends and loved ones who have gone before me?" Yet I remain silent.

At what seems to be the end of the tunnel, once again, the most immense, beautiful, warm, brilliant, radiant, loving Light shines on me and envelopes me. It's the same Light I saw when I attempted suicide. I feel awed by the beauty, peace, and serenity. Telepathically, from the Light of God, I hear, My Child, unlike the time before, you have a choice. You can come with Me or you can return and continue your life. Before you make your decision, I want to show you one more thing.

Instantly, I relive—not review, but RELIVE—my life with Jeaneen. I feel her in my womb; I feel the sensation of her first kick within me, as if it is happening in the moment. I rub my tummy, sing to her, and tell her how much I love her before she is even born. Then, I relive her actual birth, feel her tiny lips suck on my breast. I listen to her gurgles and coos. I smell the wonderful scent of my baby from her first bath. I relive numerous experiences and special times with Jeaneen throughout her twenty years. There is laughter, playfulness, and tears, as well as the challenges through our life's journey. We share moments, not only as mother and daughter, but as friends, companions, and spiritual teachers. We feel blessed to be together.

Then a spark of Light hits me, and once again, I appear before the Light of God. I'm asked, My Child, what is your decision?

The intense love, healing, and peace I feel in the Light of Infinite Spirit is so profound. Yet, I think, I can't leave Jeaneen. Not yet! *I express in sincere love, "I have to return to my daughter."*

Immediately and without warning, I'm lying in the hospital bed. My deteriorated body still looks like a skeleton, but I'm alive! Tears of joy stream down my cheeks. For the next hour, my entire Being glows with love and Light. When I close my eyes, I see bursts of Divine Light enter every cell, sparkling and vibrating with energy. The healing power of God restores me cell by cell. The sensation feels like effervescent bubbles, as if I'm being newly created with life, strength, and energy. The intense surge and vibrant life force running through me is so strong, I know before long I will be back in my earthly home, healthy!

Jeaneen comes back into the room, amazed at the transformation. "Even though you're the same person in the bed, there's much more color in your face, and you have more energy. And I see a sparkle in your eyes again." That same day we slowly walk a short distance hand in hand down the corridor. I am walking!

A few days later in meditation, I ask why I didn't see my brothers, and I hear, My Child, if you saw the one you call Tommy, your decision might have been harder. *The next day Tommy appears to me as he has in the past. He says, "Sharon, you do not have to die to be with me. I am always with you and I love you."*

Jeaneen is my heart connection and I made the right choice!

Like millions of men, women, and children, I thought suicide was the only way to find peace of mind and end my suffering. I prayed to Infinite Spirit, *If there is anything I need to know before I kill myself, let me know now.* When we call to God in time of need, our prayers are answered. They may not be answered the way we anticipate, but they will be answered for our highest good. We are never alone.

When I became infected with HIV (ARC), I was told I had six months to live if I didn't take a certain medication. At first, I bought into my doctor's death sentence. I made my doctor God.

Don't make the same mistake and give away your power. You know more about your body than anyone. The answers are all within you. Make choices that are right for you, and if you know something is wrong with your body, pursue a diagnosis.

Remember that whatever illness you may currently have, go within and listen. Perhaps it's not for your highest good to use chemotherapy or certain medications. Sometimes the treatment is worse than the disease. It's about *quality* of life, not *quantity*.

While I was in the hospital due to AIDS complications, it was important that I retained my positive attitude even though my body was dying. My daughter provided grounding for me and my love for her compelled me to come back to her.

Right after my near-death experience, as every cell in my body vibrated with Light, I came back to life with a true knowingness—at the core of my Being—that the Light of God is within me. The Light of God is *within* everyone and everything. Infinite Spirit is not outside you.

There's no fear; there's only love. That's all there is. We've become separated. We've forgotten we are one with Source, with one another, with every kingdom. We are all one with the Light and Divinity. We are all One!

I see life as a journey, a beautiful journey, that's sacred and filled with joy, with love, and with fabulous people and surroundings. I don't think you have to die to find peace or love. You can feel it through meditation, gratitude, nature, and by consciously connecting to everyone and everything. You don't have to die to reconnect.

I think one can feel a glimpse of the beauty, love, and AWE of a near-death experience by giving birth to a child. I know I did. There may be other times in your life when you felt that sacredness—a spectacular sunset, a moment with a loving pet, sweet time with a family member or friend. It's not the same as the NDE experience, but you can glimpse that connection.

It's hard if you've lost loved ones, but if you can understand that all Spirits live on, then you can always talk to your loved ones and they can hear you. Their Spirits are around; you're never truly alone.

In the mid-1980s when I worked in the AIDS community with men dying from AIDS complications, I recommended that they and their partners come up with a special signal. That way, when one of them died, he could communicate that he was fine.

Similarly, before my mom passed away, my entire family told her to make herself known during a holiday. A year after she made her transition, at Christmas, my dad, a friend, and I sat in the front room of my dad's home. Suddenly the lights went off and on three times. I felt goose bumps as my heart filled with joy. Dad and I smiled at each other. *This was the signal my mom said she would give us.* I ran into the bedroom to tell my sister and daughter, who were disappointed they didn't witness the lights blinking, although they too believed it was Mom. We took a moment to share our love for her. Since then, Mom has made her presence known to us many times.

Sometimes we are so connected, we know within our Being when something happens. When my brother Tommy died, I knew when his Spirit left his body because my heart felt heavy and I started crying. I didn't know why—I just knew something happened to him. Hours later, a friend told me Tommy was killed instantly in a motorcycle accident.

For eighteen years, Tommy came to me in Spirit form while I was both awake and asleep. Then he told me we had to let each other go. He never appeared to me again until right after my NDE.

I've learned that the veil between life and death is *so thin,* yet the invisible realm is as real or more so than the physical realm. *Just believe!*

We can learn from our experiences and become empowered, or we can become victims—real or imagined—helpless, powerless, and blaming others. An empowered person takes responsibility for his or her part, makes the most of circumstances, finds new ways to grow from challenges, and experiences inner peace. Each individual decides how to handle obstacles. I chose to live and thrive, but I needed tools.

I realized I could remain a victim or I could see all my challenges as blessings and allow them to heal me. I committed to learning various mind-body-spirit healing techniques, applying them to my life, and sharing what I learned with others. Through the process, I discovered that our greatest rewards always lie on the other side of our greatest challenges—and that out of conflict comes courage. Most important, I know we are all Beings of Love, connected to the Oneness of All.

My road to healing and peace took time and patience. Through over two decades of mind-body-spirit experiences, I learned to heal my past. By facing my challenges and releasing them, I acknowledged them as sacred. Why? Because they opened me to wholeness, helped me discover more about myself, and guided me to living my life purpose with passion. Today, my life is in harmony, balance, and peace. I can now honestly say I am truly living my life with passion!

It's never too late. The present moment is all you have. Open your eyes and heart. *Your life is waiting for you!*

There Is More . . .

Sharon is an award-winning author and documentary producer, international speaker, and has been a New Thought Minister since 1986. In April 2010, she received her Doctor of Divinity Degree from Emerson Theological Institute. She lives in beautiful San Diego, California, where she enjoys the beaches, bay, parks, and the warmth of the year-round sun. When she's not creating projects, she loves giving presentations, writing, traveling, and spending quality time with her friends and loved ones.

Active around end-of-life issues since 1986, Sharon is currently a member of San Diego County Coalition for Improving End-of-Life Care, San Diego Bereavement Consortium, International Association of Near-Death Studies, and International Association of Women Living with HIV/AIDS (ICW). To learn more about Sharon, visit SharonLund.com and SacredLife.com.

Nancy Maier
Fell Off Ladder

Nancy is a vibrant, radiant blonde with beautiful hazel eyes that capture the colors she wears. She is an artist, international speaker, spiritual practitioner, mother, and grandmother. With deep compassion and understanding, she has dedicated her life to supporting individuals in the death and dying process.

In 1975, Nancy, at thirty-two years old, was happily married with three children. Her family lived in a Midwest community and had two acres of land, including a large area for the kids to play. Nancy loved being a parent and enjoyed her creative time as an artist. "I was a happy camper."

On the cool, crisp fall day of her near-death experience, she had trimmed trees in her yard, then visited a neighbor for coffee. As she walked toward home, she noticed she'd missed trimming a large branch on one tree. She decided to climb the ladder and finish the job before it got dark. As she did, she read the printed warning on the ladder: "Do Not Stand On The Top Step." She ignored the warning and stepped onto the top step with electric shears in her hand. As she reached for the back branch, "Suddenly the ladder fell out from under me. My first concern was to get the electric shears out of the way. Then my life flashed in front of me and I blacked out." When she became conscious, she found herself lying face down on a wrought-iron chair near the tree.

She slid to the ground and could barely move. "My son was in the yard and when he saw me, he got my husband and they took me to the emergency room. The doctors couldn't find anything wrong, but decided to keep me overnight for observation because I kept feeling worse. I could hardly breathe and felt excruciating pain. I kept passing out."

The doctors finally realized that Nancy had punctured her stomach, intestines, and liver. They placed her in intensive care and before long, wheeled her into surgery.

"That's when I saw my Spirit. The essence of me looked down at my physical self lying in the hospital bed with my mom sitting next to me. Then I went through the tunnel of Light. I couldn't see my body, and I didn't feel any pain. I heard a shrill noise like a dog whistle as I tumbled around in the tunnel. I saw a lot of marvelous, pearlescent colors that changed and disappeared for what seemed like an hour but was probably seconds. Very ethereal. I felt a feeling tone of the colors. Time didn't exist. It felt as if I were going through space and I was disoriented. At the end of the tunnel, I met three Light Beings that looked like candle flames." She smiled. "I call them my welcoming committee."

These Light Beings had personalities. "I thought of them as energetic Beings and we spoke through telepathy because they have an iridescent language that's not familiar to humans. They helped me review my life. I began to experience all the discomfort I had brought upon others whom I'd hurt—I hadn't known about it before, but it made sense when I saw it from their perspectives.

"When I was back in the Earth-bound experience, I became more conscious of my actions toward people. Once you have that kind of realization, you can never go back. You have an epiphany to accommodate the new information, a knowing most people don't experience. This had a powerful spiritual effect."

The Beings asked Nancy if she wanted to stay or go back to Earth. That's when she merged with the main Light. "It was absolutely the most incredible experience of love, peace, serenity, expansive beingness, and coming-home feeling. I didn't lose my identity but merged with a greater One. I can't even begin to describe it.

"When they asked me to choose, I didn't want to come back to my Earthly experience, even though I was a mother and happily married. The Beings said it was up to me.

"I asked one question: *Would it make a difference to anyone in my family if I stayed or went back?* They said it would make a huge difference to my son, Steve, so I came back to Earth for him."

Returning to her body jolted her. "During the NDE, everything felt soft, with no hard edges." Now it felt confining in her body and she experienced a lot of pain from surgery. She knew she had made the right decision, even though she didn't want to come back.

"People told me I looked years younger after my NDE." I noticed how her countenance reflected peace. She exuded a calm feeling filled with love. "It was so wonderful. The closest thing I've experienced on this planet that we can all relate to is a climax during intercourse when you feel expanded, with a sense of free floating, total peace, and harmony with everything. No boundaries and total love."

While in the hospital, Nancy said she'd see herself in the hospital room talking to her mom and husband, then she'd go back to other realities and realms. "I went back and forth between these realms for three days. At the end of each visit, the Beings asked if I chose to stay or go back to Earth.

"I don't remember the realms very well, but each had a sensation of energy that we rarely experience here. Everything was energetic and heightened."

She added wistfully, "I'd like to explore these realms more, but I don't remember many details." However, the colors she saw and felt in the tunnel stayed with her. She now uses them in her artwork to share her experience and keep it alive. "Colors convey an unseen connection that moves between all of life," Nancy said.

After she returned to her body, Nancy experienced heightened senses. "Even though I didn't want to come back, you don't get pizza in Heaven."

The Light Beings lingered with her for almost nine months. "I felt like I knew them. They told me I would forget a lot of what I experienced because it would be difficult to integrate it into the Earthly realm. They were right.

"In our society, there was no way to frame this experience. It wasn't until I came across Raymond Moody's book, *Life After Life*, that I understood more about it. There was no one to talk to about my NDE. Now I'm wide open about discussing it, but it took me a while to get there.

"I learned that it's not what happens to us that matters, but how we respond. During my life review, I experienced the hurt and pain I caused people. It became really clear that we have to be conscious how we treat people and that we have to come from a place of love and compassion."

Nancy said her near-death experience was her greatest blessing because it started her spiritual quest in earnest. "I've always questioned traditional religions. This experience made me more open to finding my own answers that weren't restricted by dogma. I was taught Hell, fire, and brimstone, but my NDE was so wonderful, it's still amazing to me that I didn't want to come home—not even to my three young children—because of the peace, calmness, unity, expansiveness, and love I felt. The feeling goes beyond words.

"Today, I'm more open and less judging of different types of lifestyles and behaviors. There's no one right way to do things. Everything is Spirit, and I'm more of an independent thinker now than before. All is not what it seems—almost the opposite."

On her son's thirtieth birthday, the reason for her return became clear. Steve had been extremely sick and in pain for a year and a half. That day, he called her on the phone in distress. "We had talked about dying and my NDE before. When Steve had a heart attack, I held him tight. Because of my experience, I could tell him there was nothing to fear; the doors always open and close. There is nothing to be afraid of. I kept saying *It's okay to go*." Shortly after, Steve died in her arms.

"My son had birthed me into my next level of spiritual awareness the day I fell off the ladder, and I was there to birth him into his next experience beyond death. I saw his soul leave his body, and I knew where that soul was going. Even so, the feeling is bittersweet. I still miss him in the physical plane because we so enjoyed each other here."

Her son made his transition November 4, 1989. Nancy continued, "The following February while at a seminar, we were to pray for someone in our family. I had been feeling Steve's energy around me and so had his sisters. I thought perhaps he felt uncomfortable about moving on. I told my prayer partner I wanted to release my son. Then I told Steve we'd miss him, but he'd always be loved and it was all right to go. Then Steve appeared in front of me like a thin veil of Light. He showed up in a three-dimensional way, yet he was made of air, not a solid substance. He was wearing one of his favorite flannel shirts."

She smiled as she remembered how Steve used to laugh a lot. "In that moment, he laughed as only he could—*hee hee hee*—then he winked at me and vanished. Somehow, it felt so heartwarming and comforting.

"I would like people to understand that love surpasses everything, and we are all truly One. We're different, but we're all part of the same expression of the One. We're supposed to bring Heaven to Earth now, not wait until we die to experience it."

Today, Nancy lives in Kirkwood, Missouri, and contributes to a collection of stories called *Thank God I* . . . . In her story "Thank God I Died," she shares her gift of spiritual awakening.

You can read more about Nancy's life-altering NDE and her son's transition at AGlimpseOfForever.com.

Nancy is an intelligent and vibrant woman. As she climbed the ladder to trim that last branch on the tree, she read the warning sign on the top step, yet chose to take one more step and paid the price with her fall.

How many times do you see warning signs and ignore them? Know that you can find messages and signs from the Universe all around you. These symbols are placed on your path for a reason—to guide you toward your highest good, reestablish you to your birthright, and connect you to your Higher Power.

Through Nancy's experiences, we see how life can change in a heartbeat. Using her inner wisdom, she tapped into her intuition and insisted the doctors look deeper, even though they wanted to send her home from the hospital.

It's important to remember that your health remains in your hands and that, as an adult, you can accept or reject the medical treatment offered.

The two greatest gifts Nancy gave her son was giving birth to him and assisting him to make his transition with ease, grace, dignity, and love. Her compassion, love, and Light allowed him to move beyond this realm and continue his journey.

Working around end-of-life issues for many years, I've seen families cling to their loved one when it's time to set them free. Yes, it's okay to let their Spirits soar!

John Burchard
Heart Attack

John, a calm, serious man in his early 60s, says his greatest challenge in life was serving in Vietnam in the 1970s. Every Vietnam veteran I know carries many emotions about the war and John is no exception. His near-death experiences and interview were all layers of healing for him. As we talked outdoors, three hawks flew over our heads, as if holding a sacred space.

John Burchard's NDE began as he sat with his wife, Elaine, in a restaurant in March 2007. He didn't feel well and planned on visiting his doctor after they ate. Just as his wife asked if he would rather go right away, he felt a constriction in his chest. He placed his left hand over his heart in the classic heart attack gesture. Somehow, he and his wife had been fortunate enough to choose a restaurant across the street from a hospital with an emergency room. She drove them there, and when he got out of the car and couldn't walk, she carried him into the ER. At the time, John weighed 317 pounds. He still doesn't know how she managed to carry him except to say that love can do amazing things.

"They got me into the room and I died twice, once when I floated above my body and could see myself below. They brought me back, but they lost me again. The second time, I saw a place that looked like a blue crystal cave surrounded by warm love. My mother and father were there." His parents had already died.

There Is More . . .

"My mother said I could stay if I wanted, but my dad said they needed me back on Earth, that I still had much to do. I decided to go back." He then passed through a tunnel on his return to Earth and saw a silver cord that connected him to the planet. "Evidently, I was following the cord back."

When John returned to his body after the second NDE, all his senses were heightened. "I heard a nurse whispering my name, 'Mr. Burchard, Mr. Burchard,' only I heard it as a yell. I told her she had a very harsh voice!"

After recovering and finally leaving the hospital, John waited in the car as his wife stopped at a pharmacy before heading home. Amazed, he looked around, entranced by how sharp his eyesight was without glasses. "Everything looked as if it were in high definition. Also as I waited, I could smell the pavement and the sidewalk as being different from each other. I could even smell the new grass growing behind the building."

Even though he didn't receive a heart transplant (some recipients take on their donors' preferences), he noticed his tastes had changed. "I ate food that I'd hated before and didn't like some of the food I used to eat." After about three weeks, most of his senses returned to what was normal for him, but he experienced other benefits.

"I'm glad I had the near-death experiences. I'm much more tolerant of different kinds of people, and I'm also more connected to everything around me, including spiders and ants. I try not to harm anything," he says.

He suspects that he saw the blue crystal cave as a result of his upbringing. "When I was seven, my Native American grandmother began teaching me traditions of my ancestors. I studied with her for fourteen years, and part of my time with her included working with a blue crystal cave." He learned about medicine wheels, drumming circles, and other sacred teachings, many of which he doesn't share outside of his immediate family and friends. These teachings help him in his everyday life.

"My NDE helped me build on what my grandmother taught me, to respect all living things." His youngest son wanted to learn about the native traditions, so John has enjoyed passing along ancient wisdom to him.

During his recovery, John lost 91 pounds. Today, he feels stronger than ever and is eager to live life. He says he understands the human body more. "Even all our muscles breathe." His intuition and psychic abilities heightened, and he doesn't fear death. The gift of his NDEs deepened his understanding. "Life doesn't end; death is a doorway to another layer. Life goes on and on."

John continues to teach others about nature and feels a strong affinity for crystals. He leads crystal meditations for the public and offers crystal healings at various centers. In all that he does, John brings forth aspects of the Native American shaman.

Remembering his past made John's heart feel heavy when he arrived for our interview. Yet, when he shared his story and how his senses had been altered by his near-death experiences, a smile returned to his face, and he had a gleam in his eye. He confirmed that life truly is a gift—he feels as if he's been given a second chance at life. He's making the most of it by sharing his gifts and enthusiasm for crystals.

There Is More . . .

Millions of men and women around the world have had heart attacks. Unfortunately, many don't live to share their stories. When John started to experience his heart attack, he was sitting in a restaurant across the street from a hospital, evidence of Divine intervention.

John's story shows how, when we are faced with challenges, there is strength within us that can come through and accomplish the unthinkable. Miraculously, John's wife, Elaine, carried her 317-pound husband into the emergency room at the hospital.

I asked John's wife where her strength came from when she carried John. She beamed as she told me, "My strength came from the Goddess to me, in a time of need. John couldn't move and the Deity, Goddess, God, whatever name you choose, assisted me to lift him off his feet and bring him into the hospital." We all have inner strength within us and around us when it's needed. Just trust and believe.

John's attitude toward life and people changed after his NDE, but we don't have to die or experience an NDE to change our lives. Take the time to look around you now. Simple abundance, meditation, prayer, and silent time in nature can all help us reconnect to who we are inside. It doesn't take money, just a dedication to ourselves and living more abundantly with our present life.

What are you waiting for?

Alexis Burris
Pneumonia

Alexis is a middle-aged woman with sparkling green eyes. In late fall 2007, she caught pneumonia. "I couldn't catch my breath. I was coughing and, at one point, no air was coming in, and I realized I was going to die. The panic finally stopped and I heard that line out of a movie, *Today's a good day to die."*

When I asked how she felt about the experience of dying, Alexis said, "I felt grateful that it happened, though at that moment, I wasn't too thrilled about it . . . until I got to a place of surrender.

"It's an instinct to fight—fight to live, fight to breathe. It all happened very quickly, but I remember when I came to the moment when I told myself I was going to die, I saw a flash of all the things I hadn't done, all the people I hadn't talked to, how I hadn't recently told my kids I love them. It happened fast—a thousand things went through my head." Then she realized it really *was* the end. "Okay, I'm going to die, so I might as well relax into it. This is it.

"A bit later I was choking, which meant I must have relaxed enough to get in some air. I came back and I was alive again. I really didn't expect it!"

After she regained consciousness and was able to breathe, everything changed in her life. "For about the next two weeks, it was a magical time. My vision was stronger. I saw things as if everything were in high def, my vision was so clear. I only slept about three hours a night. I was loaded with energy, happy as a clam. I'd be up at three o'clock in the morning trimming the

There Is More . . .

hedges quietly so I wouldn't wake up the neighbors. I got into a ritual where, as the sun came up, I would play a Paul Potts CD, drink a glass of Champagne, and watch the Earth wake up." Her eyes looked dreamy and far away as she recalled that time.

"I know we only have five senses but it felt like I had thirty!" Right after her near-death experience, she felt unplugged from all the problems and stresses of everyday life. "Then gradually I fell back into a feeling of day-to-dayness. But it was definitely the happiest time of my life. I like to remember it to get back into that space again and lighten up."

Alexis now has a better sense of well-being than before. "I know this is all meant to be good. And if not, it's my creation. So I guess it's more freeing that way because I know if I want to make myself miserable, I'm fully capable of it. But that wasn't the plan."

She doesn't think that we each have one life purpose. "Our purpose is about what we do with our feelings more than the things we do or have. It's about joy and our connection to the whole."

This wasn't Alexis's first encounter with death. In 1989, she worked with a 24-year-old man, Jon, her design assistant. "He had movie-star good looks, and he also had AIDS," she recalled wistfully. "I hadn't seen him in a long time, but I knew he'd been in the hospital."

One night at home as she walked from her bedroom toward the staircase, ". . . a huge blast of energy, both wind and Light, hit me, throwing me against the wall. I had to hold onto the banister so I wouldn't fall over."

Confused, she shut her eyes against the Light, but her eyelids glowed with the intense colors around her: blue/white with yellow, pink and red. Somehow, she realized the energy felt like her assistant, Jon.

In that moment, she and Jon connected on a telepathic, energetic level. He was totally confused, and neither one of them knew why he was there. Alexis could hear his voice in her left ear and another voice in her right ear, saying, *Tell him to walk to the Light.* She realized she was a conduit, a bridge between the spiritual realm and wherever Jon was at the moment. She was connecting them like an extension cord.

Alexis passed on the message to Jon. "Walk to the Light." He argued in her left ear, yet the voice of guidance continued in her right. Alexis kept her eyes closed against the intense Light, but could see shadowy forms coming up to meet him. She didn't recognize the voice of guidance in her right ear. "It really wasn't about me; it was about him. I could tap into the frequency easier than he could, so I got to help him."

Then suddenly the energy, the Light, the voices, all disappeared. She found herself in her living room thinking "Wow!"

Alexis learned later that Jon was in the process of dying in the hospital that night. His Spirit had probably already separated; his body had died about six hours after their strange middle-of-the-night encounter. She still thinks of that night as if she were a coach helping Jon cross over to the other side. She feels honored to have assisted.

Alexis continues to be a successful artist, businesswoman, and entrepreneur. She currently sells 'Simple Greeting' cards at Whole Foods in San Diego and elsewhere, as well as through

SimpleGreetingCards.net. You can see her paintings at AlexisBurris.com.

Alexis is a delight. She exudes energy, joy, and love for life. Just being in her presence lifts my spirits.

Sometimes people don't remember the actual event, but experience the side effects of their NDE. Alexis is one of these. Though she blacked out when she ran out of oxygen, she came back renewed, happy, and the heightened senses and other side effects lasted for days. Some persist years later.

When Alexis was dying from pneumonia and fighting for her last breath, she released control and surrendered to the process, thinking, "I'm going to die." Then she relaxed into it. Her decision to not fight allowed her to breathe again. In a sense, she let go and let God.

Alexis saw a flash of things she hadn't done or said such as, "I haven't told my kids lately that I love them." Sometimes we get so caught up in our daily lives that we forget what's really important.

For example, waking up in the morning is often taken for granted. Alexis shows us the pure joy of watching the morning come to life—a daily miracle that most of us miss. Alexis also shows us that it's our choice if we make our lives miserable because we are responsible for our thoughts, feelings, and actions.

Take time to acknowledge the people in your life and what you find meaningful. Remember that you are a gift to the world. What are you holding back that you can share?

Let your Light shine brightly.

Alexis had a deep connection with Jon and felt his Spirit around her as he was making his transition. Open to hearing that his Spirit needed to be guided, she was blessed and honored to assist him in walking toward the Light.

Perhaps someday you'll be called on to assist others while they make their transition or go toward the Light. You will be blessed by it, and so will they.

Jil Streed
Trapped in Wildfire

October 2007 was another month of infamy for California. Four years earlier, over two thousand homes were lost in the San Diego area in one week when wildfires, fueled by Santa Ana winds, raced across the landscape. Residents thought tragedy would only hit once. They were wrong.

Jil, a middle-aged jewelry artist with a home in the backcountry, was caught in the fire of 2007. She felt isolated, confused, and uncertain about what really happened.

Jil knew the wildfire was bearing down on her rural home that October day. She drove her truck and horse trailer down a windy two-lane road toward the back of her neighbor's property where she planned on picking up her horses and taking them to safety. She drove past the fire station where people seemed unconcerned about the low fire eating up the brush. As she drove, though, the fire grew bigger and faster, and Jil tried to outrun the flames. It didn't work.

"The fire was off to the right and the wall of flames got huge, and then I was engulfed in flames. All I could see was black and red, with big chunks of charcoal flying past, and smoke coming into the truck." There was so much smoke, the truck's engine choked. "I realized I couldn't take my foot off the accelerator pedal or I would die. I had to floor it to keep the truck running. I was terrified."

As she continued to speed down the windy street, "I saw a vision of myself crashed on the side of the road. I'd somehow crawled outside of the truck and I saw myself black and crispy, and my husband was standing over my body mourning.

"I couldn't let that happen to him. I couldn't let my husband find me that way. That gave me the strength to keep going and I grabbed the steering wheel."

Then her dogged determination shifted. She looked around the cab and something came over her. "Suddenly, it didn't matter anymore. I felt bliss and happiness—I knew nothing bad was going to happen to me." Inside the cab, she was surrounded by a bluish Light, like a blue/white tunnel. "It was beautiful! There I was, speeding down a windy road, my truck surrounded by flames, and I felt no fear."

As she continued driving, she saw a vision of forearms coming through the windshield and grabbing her arms just below her elbows, as if helping her steer through the fire. "It looked to be a whitish form and I felt it was an angel. The most amazing thing is I just let go in the moment and abandoned all thoughts of control." Then a few seconds later, her truck was on the other side of the fire, and she was safe.

"I escaped the flames just beyond where I had to make a left turn to get to my neighbor's house. I slumped forward while driving and was gasping for air. I noticed a Highway Patrol officer at the corner who was preventing people from driving into the area that I had just miraculously made it through. The look on his face was one of shock and horror.

"I made it to our neighbor's house and sped into the driveway, stopped the truck, and jumped out. I looked around the truck and in the engine for fire. I suddenly felt weak and bent over. My husband was at my neighbor's house and came over to help. The wheel cover of the spare tire was charred and the whole right side of the truck had wax melted off. The horse trailer had scorch marks.

"The fire went around our properties, then there was a huge glow to the east of us. It was now burning straight toward our house and the neighbor's house. Fire personnel told us to leave. In total shock, I saw hundred-foot flames race up the hill, curling violently like a wave covering from one end of our neighborhood to the other. Smoke instantly became so thick that we couldn't see the fire vehicle only twenty-five feet from us." They had to leave the horses, truck, and trailer. They jumped into their little car that her husband had driven down the horse trail to the neighbor's house.

"With our dog in the back seat, we sped away and could barely see in front of the car. Debris, embers, smoke, and fallen trees littered the road. The second escape was just as terrifying as the first because we didn't know if the roads would be open or if we were driving into a worse situation—we just knew we couldn't stay.

"We somehow managed to reach our small rural highway. There, fire blocked us, so we sat in our car for about three hours, blown around by hurricane-force winds from the fire. Our old dog was coughing and we were worried he would die. We watched helplessly in horror as our whole neighborhood became consumed by flames. We even saw the glow of our house burning.

"Finally, we were directed to proceed to the Intermountain Fire Department down the road where we stayed the rest of the night with other escapees.

"We later got confirmation from a neighbor that our house was burned to the ground. I was in total shock and felt nauseous from the news. We couldn't sleep that night. In the morning, we ventured home to see what was left. Driving up to our property was like visiting the moon; the scorched wasteland smelled horrible and things were still burning. I can't describe the feeling we had standing next to the ashes of our once-beautiful house."

When Jil saw only the ashes and rubble of her home, she couldn't believe so much could be reduced to so little in such a short time. She's an artist and all her work, all her tools, all her worldly possessions were lost, with the exception of their pets and their car, truck, and trailer.

Jil's smile looked bittersweet as she recalled what happened next. "There was a moment of sadness and then a sense of *overwhelming freedom* came over me! It was a feeling I had wanted to experience on Earth my whole life—a *freedom* from *material objects*."

She realized that, even before the fire, "I really needed to change how I live."

After the fire, Jil was eager to tell her family and friends about her experience with the blue Light and how an angel helped her through. However, no one wanted to hear about it. She felt confused and isolated. She had never met anyone who understood what she went through until our interview. In October 2009, she attended the International Association of Near-Death Studies (IANDS) Annual Conference in San Diego. There, she made friends and felt comfortable sharing her story. Now, she feels more validated.

Two years after the fire, her home is finally rebuilt and her life somewhat back to normal, but her near-death experience has stayed with her. She feels a bit disconnected, as if caught between two worlds. "I'm trying to embrace being on Earth, but

I don't know how to assimilate my new awareness. I need to find a way to simplify my life in my own way."

Jil has been creating jewelry since 1972. Her beautiful handcrafted pieces combine free-spirited inspiration balanced by sophisticated, timeless design.

"My jewelry is a vehicle to opening or deepening spirituality. Customers often select jewelry based on their connection to the title of the piece. This becomes their personal affirmation, a private and spiritual journey. It is a constant reminder of their journey."

Jil uses high quality semi-precious gemstones to enhance her sterling silver collection. To view her merchandise, visit JilStreed.com.

Jil became visibly more vibrant as she shared her experience with me. She found someone who listened and cared about what happened to her, and someone who had experienced a similar spiritual situation.

If you don't find the support you need, don't shut down. Keep seeking a connection with others because there are people somewhere who care and understand. Remember that God is within you, so you can always turn within to find comfort. As Jil increasingly feels comfortable sharing her NDE, she will become brighter and lighter.

While Jil drove her truck through the wildfire, she released control and an angel helped her drive. When she surrendered, she felt a sense of peace and joy, like nothing bad could happen to her. What would it take for you to release control in a desperate situation?

Imagine having your beautiful home and all your possessions reduced to ashes. Could you lose every worldly possession and still find a deeper peace within yourself, a part of yourself richer and brighter than anything in the material world?

Remember, we aren't our worldly possessions. We are Spiritual Beings who sometimes get so caught up in the material world, we forget who we are and what is truly important. When you release your attachment to the outcome, greater things can happen.

What can you release now that will allow your Spirit to soar? Codependency? Too many physical belongings? Responsibilities that aren't yours? The only chains on your mind and Spirit are the ones you attach there.

✧
Dan Schaff
MRSA (Staph Infection)

Dan always believed in Heaven and Higher Powers. As far back as he can recall, his mom preached to him, "Every day there will be a challenge, and God doesn't expect you to pass them all, but he does expect you to try."

At an early age, Dan understood what needed to be done to succeed in everything that was put in front of him. That included the war in Vietnam, and his sister's death.

He remembers being extremely angry at God and the Catholic Church. He chose to turn his back on both when his dad's best friend, a priest, wouldn't bury his sister at their local church because she had lived in a different city five miles away. Dan had looked at his dad and screamed at the priest, "That's bullshit."

His dad replied in anger, "You shouldn't talk to people that way." Then Dan said, "Having your best friend refuse to do a favor for you is the biggest bullshit." After that, he didn't want anything to do with the Catholic Church or God.

Years later, a man from the mortuary talked to Dan about his beliefs about God. When Dan told him the story about the priest, the man said, "Don't be mad at God, it's the man representing God who made that choice."

Dan burst into tears. His crying then allowed him to start his grief cycle for his sister.

Dan shared his story with me from a chair in the examination room at the San Diego County Medical Examiner's Office. Not only was it Friday the thirteenth, but a stiff rain pelted San Diego, a city that normally receives little moisture. This night, however, was different.

Dan seemed like a warm Teddy bear in a cold sterile facility filled with a smell of metal, formaldehyde, and decay. The people working there don't seem to mind the smell. I breathed through it and took a quick tour, complete with seeing bodies in the cooler. I noticed stacks of body bags on shelves against the wall. Nearby rested an empty gurney as well as a gurney in the hallway laden with an embalmed body inside a bag.

Surrounded by shiny stainless steel cabinets, tables, and sinks, Dan and I sat down to talk.

A mortician since he returned from Vietnam in the mid-1970s, Dan deals with the death of others every day; however, on July 30, 2006, he had his own near-death experience. As he talked, he took a deep breath and tears welled up in his eyes.

"I had three wounds that wouldn't heal and several days of what seemed like the flu. Finally, I couldn't get out of bed, and I knew I had to get to the hospital or I would die. My wife Barbara drove me to the emergency room, and the triage nurse gave me morphine and an IV.

"While I sat in a wheelchair, she kept taking my blood pressure, then talking to me, taking my blood pressure, and talking to me. I asked what she was doing." After she gave him an offhand excuse about pain medication, he said, "I'm a mortician, don't sugar this or anything." She admitted that with such low blood pressure, he shouldn't even be able to talk. Then she took his blood pressure once more and grabbed the wheelchair. "It was almost like smoke and fire coming off the wheels as she raced me into the emergency room screaming, 'We need a bed! We need a bed! We need a bed now!' When an ER doctor asked her why, she said, 'His blood pressure is seventy over sixty and I'm losing him!'

"That's when . . . they lost me. I was sucked through a wall into a light blue-gray waiting room about ten by twelve. It had chairs, one door, and a trash can next to the door. As soon as I walked past that trash can . . . everything was gone."

His eyes teared and he choked up as he spoke. "My worries, my concerns, and my pain, was gone. I felt really good. There was nothing but happiness." He counted six chairs in the room. Then something like a speaker box asked him to be seated. While he sat and waited, he could hear the nurses and doctors say, "Give him oxygen; give him another IV; we need to get him up on the bed."

Dan continued, "The room felt peaceful and smelled like a toss-up between my mom's kitchen and cookies and lilacs and roses." Tears kept flowing as he remembered the details.

He described sitting in the waiting room singing to himself and praying, thanking God for 'letting me graduate.'

"I also thanked God for letting me do what I did, and hoped I had fulfilled my obligations. I'll get to go fishing with my dad again," he explained, because his dad had passed away years before.

Dan kept praying and humming his favorite song "I Am Free" by the Who, which he sings whenever he graduates from something. Suddenly the waiting room door opened and a short figure of a man entered. Behind the man, Dan could see the radiant Light he assumed was the tunnel everyone talks about. All he could see was the Light outlining the silhouette of the man who said, "Danny, we're sending you back."

"Why? I couldn't believe it. I was ready to die, relieved to be free of my earthly burdens. After all, I'd graduated. Why would they pull my ticket?"

"You're still needed really badly back there, Danny."

Only three people ever called him "Danny," one of them his pastor, an elderly man who had died the previous night.

Dan still didn't understand. He wanted clarification. As he asked for an explanation, he got to "Wh . . ." when he felt a shock of electricity. He found himself back in his body in the emergency room, talking to the nurse.

"You staying with us this time?" she asked.

"I don't have any control over that, but I don't want any more of that electricity. Did you guys shock me?"

"No, but that's why I'm asking." Dan noticed a nurse in the corner rubbing the paddles together in case they had to shock him back to life.

"How long was I gone?"

"Long enough. Daniel, we have bigger things to worry about right now, like keeping you alive. Let me concentrate on what I'm doing." They put him to sleep for a while and kept him in intensive care.

The next morning, several doctors arrived and one said, "You're a very, very, very, very sick man."

Dan replied, "Yeah, I know. My friends tell me that all the time."

"Even this close to death, you have a sense of humor?" The doctor seemed amazed.

Dan smiled. "I been there, Doc, and it doesn't matter."

The medical team diagnosed him with MRSA, a potentially deadly staph infection. After massive doses of antibiotics, he finally got to go home, but to this day, his body hurts all the time. It feels as if he's been in a car accident, and he suspects the medics may have dropped him while moving him at the hospital.

Dan does believe he's needed here on Earth. His teenage son had gone through hard times with drugs, but once he saw Dan in the hospital with tubes in him, "My son realized something on his part needed to be dealt with. Now he hugs me and holds me again and says he loves me." Tears filled Dan's eyes and he could barely talk as he shared this part of his journey. "That's something I'd missed for three years."

Today, Dan feels devastated that he was forced to come back to his body. He's tired of the "everyday Wiley Coyote ride." Everything felt good when he left his body, but now he's in constant pain. Yet since his NDE, he has a lot more patience with people and spends more time with his family. He finds he has less tolerance for stupid, petty conflicts that waste time. However, he realizes all the circumstances that come into life happen for a reason. He can always choose how he reacts to them.

"God is in my life every day and He keeps me going. I'm not a religious person as far as going to church. God is with me and so are my guardian angels and Jesus."

There Is More . . .

During his NDE, he recalls, "I got to go on the up elevator instead of the down elevator, and it was wonderful, wonderful, wonderful. There's no way of explaining, no vocabulary, about how great it is just to be there."

The longing in his voice tore at my heart. Dan continued, "I wish I could go back. I hope they have motorcycles and long freeways there. People may feel peace and love in their hearts and minds here, but there's absolutely no comparison or words to describe what it felt like there."

After dealing with death as a mortician since 1974, Dan had a chance to see firsthand what it's all about. "I sat in the waiting room of Heaven. I saw the Light, smelled the smell, and felt the feeling. Every time I tell this story, I know someone is with me up there."

Dan continues to work at the San Diego County Medical Examiner's Office as a mortician. On his days off, he enjoys riding his motorcycle and spending time with his family.

Dan is a man whose presence warmed my heart and Spirit. His humor is contagious and his sensitivity runs deep.

As a mortician working at the medical examiner's office, Dan works around death and dead bodies daily. However, he had the opportunity to experience that he is not his body.

In the NDE, Dan also found an interesting connection to his late father. Years before, his dad had telephoned Dan and asked,

"Why does it hurt so badly when you come back from death to living?"

Dan explained that we are a positive force and the Earth a negative force. When the Spirit comes back into the body, it crosses over like an arcing battery. This was the same feeling Dan had when he returned to his body.

Then his dad asked him, "Why does God keep sending me back?"

"Sending you back? When did you die?"

His dad told him he died twice and God told him each time he had to go back. The last time happened in 2004 at a Thanksgiving party—his dad just finished dinner and bent over to tie his shoelace when he collapsed. The medical team brought him back to life at the hospital. He told Dan his Spirit lifted out of his body and many people waved him on, but he was told he had to go back.

Dan was surprised and shocked that his dad had never mentioned this before. When Dan asked why he kept it to himself, his dad explained, "Daniel, I live in North Dakota, and when a person talks about flying saucers or near-death experiences, everyone thinks that person is crazy."

Dan asked him why he didn't at least talk to his best friend, the priest, about it, and again his response was, "Because it's North Dakota."

Then Dan attempted to comfort his dad and told him that hundreds of thousands of people experience NDEs. "There's no reason not to talk about it."

Knowing all this, Dan felt a deeper connection to his dad on a different level than ever before because they have NDEs in common. They both know what it's like to be in the Light, enjoying peace and immense love.

Our bodies are sacred vehicles that allow us to experience and express ourselves on this life plane. We are magnificent Spiritual Beings much more than we are physical bodies.

Dan was forced to come back into his body because he was needed on Earth. We all have gifts to share and are needed by someone, even if we're not aware of that person.

No one knows how or when we will breathe our last precious breath. The present moment is all we have. Let's live each one to the fullest.

Carla Jean Tooker
Diabetic Coma

For Carla, a soft-spoken, middle-aged woman with blonde hair and big lovely eyes, her life before her NDE had lost intellectual stimulation, and her relationship with her boyfriend was not healthy. She worked in a restaurant and when she started working behind the bar, the atmosphere made it easy to drink away her troubles.

"Being around alcohol became a symptom of my unhappiness."

About that time, her beloved young son had gone to live with his father. "When my husband and I split up, it was not pleasant. I think my son felt torn between my husband and me, and he started acting out. He needed the presence of his dad, so I made a heart-wrenching decision to let him live with his father.

"I really missed my son's playfulness, spirit, and love."

On July 4, 1992, Carla decided to quit drinking, but after a few days, realized she needed help to do so. She went to rehab and the people there immediately sent her to the hospital. She was so dehydrated, the nurse had problems locating a vein to start IV treatments. After testing, they realized she was in critical condition and rushed her into intensive care. She plunged into a diabetic coma for eight days, plagued with a multiple array of problems, several of them life-threatening.

While in the coma, Carla found herself in a tunnel of Light. "It was so loving, peaceful, and welcoming." She remembers being surrounded by four angels who slowly walked her down the

There Is More . . .

tunnel. They came to a crossing, looked at Carla lovingly and said, "You have to make a choice right now whether you want to come with us, and you're welcome to, or you can go back."

At that moment, Carla screamed out, "I want to live, I want to live!" The doctor and her ex-boyfriend, standing at her bedside, heard her yell those exact words.

She was suddenly sucked back out of the tunnel and immediately regained consciousness.

With a smile on her face and a sparkle in her eyes, she told me, "It was very tempting to stay. The feeling was so welcoming."

Carla noted that after her NDE, she saw the world with new eyes. "It was like I was a baby because I was so fragile and didn't have physical strength. Yet I was happy, happy just to be alive." After a month in the hospital, she came out with a diagnosis of diabetes. That's when she realized she needed to start her life over in a new location. "Leaving the hospital with a new disease, and the fear of managing it while starting a new life, was overwhelming."

She said she had forgotten all the years of destruction that had gotten her to that point. She woke up with a new sense of life, self, and direction. "It was as if any bad karma was left behind in my NDE. All my past burdens lifted." Her mother and fourteen-year-old son encouraged her to share her experience with them. "They saw a tremendous change in me and wanted to hear what I remembered. Telling them what happened helped me reconnect with them."

Carla's senses were heightened a bit, and for the first few months, when she wore a watch, it would stop working within a matter of minutes. She also had to be careful when visiting a friend who lived near the beach. "At sunset, the sunlight on the water made such a pathway of light, it reminded me of the tunnel. I had to be careful I didn't stare and get lost in it while I was driving."

With confidence and peace, she stated, "I'm not afraid to die anymore. I know it to be a loving, warm, happy place, so it doesn't scare me."

Carla's self-image changed and she felt as if she came back home. "I could see the self I'd lost and that was an absolutely wonderful thing for me. I'd forgotten how far off track I'd gotten." She knew she wanted a new life and was warned by doctors that any introduction of alcohol into her body would bring back body memory—and death. Clearly, her life depended on healthy choices.

Although she now has to deal with diabetes every day, it's a daily reminder to take care of herself. "Life is now wonderful, healthy, happy, and full."

"Six years after my NDE, I was diagnosed with breast cancer. I wasn't afraid to die—I didn't want to die, but I felt no fear. My treatment went well, and I live each day in Love. It's the core of my life."

She continues to call on her angels, especially during times of stress or danger. "I also trust my intuition more."

Carla got breast cancer and finished chemotherapy treatments in 1999. She has been cancer free ever since.

Today, Carla shares her love with others. She works for Meals on Wheels, providing food to homebound people in San Diego.

There Is More . . .

"I love my job," she smiles, her joy filling the room, her happiness contagious.

At first, Carla felt uncomfortable talking about her past. However, once she understood that her story can make a difference in people's lives, she felt exhilarated and wanted to share because her message is so powerful and her challenges so common.

Early in life, Carla's choices and behaviors brought her to the doorway of death. However, her will to live made her shout, "I want to live! I want to live!" Her cry was heard and her wishes respected. She returned to her body, her Spirit healed. Since that day, she has lived well, with gratitude and love.

When you call upon Infinite Spirit, you will receive a response. Ask for help out loud.

Carla had a Spiritual Awakening and understood how far off track she'd become with her life. Like a rebirth, her NDE gave her the ability to live life in joy. She no longer felt the need to avoid life by abusing her body.

Love and nurture your body, a sacred vessel. It carries you through this lifetime, allowing you to feel all the emotions so you can choose how to respond, how to enhance your experiences, and whom to love. Allow your body to carry you through this lifetime the best it can, and if you have physical ailments, realize they may help teach you something vital about yourself. What has your body already taught you? How have you responded to your body? Have you nurtured it today?

Helen Wendle
Suicide Attempt

Helen's radiant, blue eyes sparkled like diamonds. She told me in her soft voice that she'd lived the rich and famous lifestyle. She and her second husband had owned a twenty-two-room home on a fifteen-acre estate, an island in Florida, a private jet, and several expensive cars. They employed a captain for their yacht, a full time housekeeper and butler, and seemed to take all this opulence for granted.

"Spending money meant nothing. It was just something we did because we could, but money isn't everything. It doesn't buy happiness like so many people think it does. Something wasn't right in my second marriage, but I didn't know until later what it was," Helen told me.

She used to live in New York with her first husband and two sons. "My first husband became an alcoholic and was abusive to me and my younger son, but he kept my older son on a pedestal." She tried to hold things together, but her life was like a nightmare. "One time, I was in my studio painting and for no apparent reason, my husband grabbed me by my hair, dragged me down the stairs, and tried to thrust my head into the gas oven. Another time, he told me he was going to kill me, but not the children. He spat in my face and constantly degraded me. The abuse went on for years and I didn't have the courage to divulge what went on behind closed doors to my parents or anyone else. We had firearms in the house so that scared me, too. Many nights I'd lie in bed shaking and fearing for my life."

After being together seventeen years, Helen divorced her first husband. She and her two children experienced a lot of stress, especially the youngest. When she was thirty-eight years old, her youngest son jumped out of her car while she drove him through an industrial part of New York. "I was scared—I didn't know where he went. I looked everywhere and he was nowhere in sight."

Feeling scared and hopeless, Helen drove home and cried. She'd had it with life! "I wanted to die." She'd never thought of hurting herself before, but that day, she put her old VW in the garage, shut the door, and with the motor running, she started to pray.

Then she realized she needed to write a note to her children and parents, telling them they weren't to blame for her suicide. She just couldn't go on any longer.

"I had the old VW running in our one-car garage and a lot of fumes built up. I wrote my note, then returned to the car, sat in the driver's seat, and prayed to Jesus. I repeated the Hail Mary and Our Father over and over, asking Him to please forgive me for what I was about to do. Then I realized I had one more thing to add to my farewell note." She stumbled out of the car, opened the kitchen door, and collapsed.

"My Spirit went through a long dark tunnel. It was really dark, but I wasn't frightened. In fact, I felt calm and at peace. I remember going through that tunnel and then hitting a bright, radiant Light. I felt peace from it, no fear. A voice, I think Jesus, said, *Go back, you have more to do.* It was so peaceful. It happened quickly. I had no sense of time. I felt joy throughout my Being and immersed myself in the Light for a while. It took time to get back into my body." She continued to feel that peace when she returned to her body.

She says, "There is something out there stronger then we can imagine. When I was in the car in the garage, I prayed to Jesus, asking him to forgive me for what I was doing. I believe Jesus saved me."

The next thing Helen remembered was her runaway son and her parents finding her on the kitchen floor. "I actually don't remember seeing my family, but I know they were there. I do remember my father gently touching my head and saying in a loud, nervous voice, like he was crying, 'Helen, what happened? What happened?'"

Helen cried as she shared with me how happy she felt to be alive. "My prayers were answered. God saved me. He guided my son and parents there at the right time."

She spent two days in the hospital, her mother at her side day and night. The doctor said that when the paramedics reached her, she was minutes away from death and her lips were turning blue. "The doctor told me the x-rays were clear. I was lucky. I didn't have any damage to my lungs. He said if I ever tried to commit suicide again, I would succeed."

Her suicide attempt seems like a selfish act to her now. She's genuinely happy to be alive.

"When the police came to the house, a police officer took my suicide note. But after I was released from the hospital a few days later, this officer came to my home to see how I was doing and handed me the note. I remember crying and telling him how grateful I was to be alive and thanking him. He was an angel because he didn't report my suicide attempt. I think I put the note under the mattress but I never found it again. It's a mystery where it ended up.

There Is More . . .

"For years I never spoke of my suicide attempt. I was concerned what people would think of me." Today, she looks at life differently. "I'm honest, strong, confident, and wise. I don't care what people think of me. I'm more in touch with human beings and their feelings, with the world itself and being alive. We all experience good and bad times. It's part of being human.

"My son and I never talked about what happened—he was an angry boy because his father was so abusive and threatening. My first husband is deceased now, but he eventually stopped drinking and we got to be friends the last few years."

Through Helen's healing, she learned the importance of forgiveness. "My ex-husband helped me out financially a lot before he died, I think because he felt so guilty about how he treated me. I truly hope he is at peace. I hold no animosity toward him. Basically, he was a good person and the father of my two wonderful sons, whom I am proud of and love dearly."

It still wasn't easy, though. Helen had a mental breakdown and wasn't able to spend some of that time with her boys, but life is better now. "I know I'm safe and God is here to help me regardless of what situation I'm going through. I appreciate life more now. I'm more outgoing than I was. I've opened up. I didn't want to die."

She planned on staying single, using her art talent to create paintings for art galleries, private collectors, and custom artwork for the Ethan Allen galleries. Then one night, about five years after her divorce from her husband, Helen was driving over the George Washington Bridge on a fall evening and prayed out loud, "Dear God, please send a kind and special gentleman into my life." She met her second husband that night—a spontaneous attraction. They got married and she enjoyed a wealthy lifestyle, but something seemed wrong.

Helen Wendle

It nagged at her.

"We had a happy life, and only had two arguments in our twelve years together. However, I knew something wasn't right." Her second marriage turned to tragedy when her husband finally told her he had lung cancer and was dying. "I thought it was a joke when he told me he only had five years to live. After he died, I tried to contact him every day and night. He promised me he'd give me a sign that he was okay when he passed on to the other side. About three weeks after I tried to first communicate with him, images of doves flew into my room; there must have been a hundred of them. I followed one dove. It went to the window and a transparent image of a face appeared—my husband's. I think he was telling me he was okay. I think he's in a better place."

Even though her second husband had been wealthy and had assured Helen she'd be financially secure, he left her penniless. "It was a shock. I was never involved with his businesses, but he reassured me my finances would be okay. That was the part of him I didn't know."

She had to start her life over again, but as hard as it was, "I had the tools to begin again because the power of God is within me. No matter how hard things get, my faith is remarkably strong. I'd never attempt suicide again. It's a selfish act and it hurts the people you leave behind—family and friends. I get through day by day, one day at a time."

Helen smiled and explained that even though she lost her money and all her possessions, she's happier than ever before. "Life is a gift and time is precious, not to be wasted."

She now lives in a home no larger than a two-car garage she can hardly pay for, yet it's the happiest time of her life. She's free

There Is More . . .

from material possessions. "I now have a sense of peace and harmony for everything and everyone."

Helen had never thought about death much before, ". . . but now I don't fear it. Everyone's going to die. It's not up to us when. We're put on this Earth for a reason.

"When my mom passed away, I looked up at the sky and cried, and saw the clouds create the form of an angel. I believe that was her sign to me." She smiled. "God puts Earth angels in your life and I know I have several in mine. Doors open with people I meet. There are a lot of angels out there, living and spiritual. I hope I can reciprocate and become someone's angel in a time of need. It doesn't cost anything to be helpful or put a smile on someone's face.

"I've had the opulent life of the rich and famous, but I know that peace of mind is more important than anything. I don't want material items anymore—I want to be free like a bird."

She laughed, "How many cups do you need?"

Helen continues to live free as a bird and enjoys creating her artwork. She's writing a book about her life story titled *Hel N: What a Ride*. She enjoys visiting her two sons and grandchildren on the east coast as often as she can.

Helen lives with confidence, grounded and centered in her truth.

Through Helen's experience, we see that when she attempted suicide, it was no accident that her son and parents arrived in time to save her life. The Universe sets things up, and a Higher Power weaves its influence through our lives.

Helen shifted from an abusive relationship to a loving one, and though she didn't know about her second husband's mystery around financial wealth, her intuition told her something wasn't right—that he carried some secret. Then he died of cancer and left her penniless.

When things don't go your way, perhaps that path wasn't for your highest good, or was simply a life lesson.

When Helen was no longer living the life of the "rich and famous" and struggled financially, she felt liberated from responsibility for all her "things" and connected deeply to her inner God Source. When we die, we leave all our material possessions behind anyway. What good are they to us when we already have all we desire, a full heart and sense of bliss?

Helen attempted to contact her second husband after he made his transition. Her prayers were answered as images of doves flew into her room and the face of her husband appeared; she then knew he was at peace and in a better place. Doves symbolize peace—how appropriate!

Before your loved ones make their transitions, ask them to give you a sign, symbol, or way to communicate with you and let you know they are fine. Be open to seeing, hearing, and believing—it can happen to you.

Helen also realized she has all the tools she needs to succeed in life because they are all within her. All of us have the tools within us!

There Is More . . .

Throughout her journey, Helen met Earth angels. Do you recognize your Earth angels? Do you acknowledge your Earth angels? Are you available to others as their Earth angel?

Scott Borowik
Car Accident

Scott is a quiet, handsome man, six-foot-one with blue eyes and salt-and-pepper hair. He loves the outdoors, especially surfing and hiking. Before his NDE, he had a stable job working for a photo lab for two-and-a-half years.

Part of the day of Scott's near-death experience he can vividly remember, but the rest, he knows only by what people have told him. Here's what he told me.

"In the summer of 1984, two friends and I were on a surfing trip in Baja, California. It was hot and there wasn't much surf. We got in the water, did a little surfing, and then stopped off at the Half Way House for some food. While we were there, we each drank a couple of margaritas. As we walked out to the car, I felt loopy and knew I was in no condition to drive. My friend assured me he was fine and grabbed the keys to drive my car. I sat in the passenger seat of my 1968 white VW square back. The other guys sat in back.

"As soon as the car engine started, I dozed off. My friend drove along the coast road, which was one lane each direction north and south. The next thing I remember, I was lying on the highway with the left side of my face on the asphalt, moaning, 'Please dear God, let me sleep.' At that moment everything changed."

Scott didn't remember anything after his prayer to God until hours later when he was told he was in a hospital in Tijuana. "People hovered over me and were screaming, 'We're going to get you out of here!' I couldn't see the details of faces, I just heard sounds. I didn't comprehend what was going on. I was only aware of people saying, 'Help is coming, help is coming.'"

They took Scott and the other injured people across the United States border by ambulance. "The next thing I remember, I was put into a helicopter. I was told I had the most internal injuries so Life Flight flew me to UCSD Medical Center. The sound of the rotating helicopter blades was intense."

Scott remembers arriving at the medical center where people wheeled him around. "I recall them taking me out of the helicopter while I was out of my body watching the situation. My body lay on a gurney and my Spirit helped the trauma team push it through the emergency entrance and into the operating room. It was like 3-D. I saw myself and the people around me. I participated with my own care. It was peaceful and amazing. My Spirit was calm, knowing they were going to operate on my body. I didn't feel any pain or see myself as a bloody gory mess. I couldn't see any details; I just felt peace as I looked at my body below.

"That was my last recollection until hours or days later. I'm not sure about time. In the next state of consciousness, I was shooting through a bright tunnel of Light, feet first. I felt like I was shaking, like riding in a jet or a spaceship. A force pushed me through the tunnel of Light, faster than the speed of sound.

"I came into a room and I didn't see anyone, just a clock. I thought, *I'm still here, I'm still alive.* That was the struggle, going between this world and the next. It wasn't my time to die. The clock, whether in my imagination or not, was two or three in the morning. I remember feeling cold, really cold."

When Scott came back into his body, his heart was racing and he felt palpitations. "The NDE was so peaceful and powerful. Nothing was frightening except the intensity of coming back into my body. It would be amazing to experience what's at the end of the journey through the tunnel."

For the next several hours, Scott experienced traveling back and forth through the tunnel of Light. He had the same sensations and outcome of traveling at rapid speed, seeing the clock, and then coming back, conscious, in his body. Although it seemed like days or weeks, only a few hours had passed.

"It felt as if I went through a portal but I didn't get to the end. It was taking me somewhere but I didn't get to see what was on the other side. It was like traveling on an unfamiliar road and not knowing where it's taking you—toward the forest or the ocean.

"I sense there's another place we go to after here. The soul, Spirit, whatever you want to call it, moves on to the next incarnation. I believe that was what was going on in the hospital. I was getting ready to take the next journey but it wasn't time."

Every time Scott came back into his body, he was alone. While telling me this, he had a confused look on his face. "I felt alone in the world. My body was ice cold."

He learned later he was fighting an infection and the doctors wanted to keep his fever down so they didn't allow him to have blankets.

"After the initial experience, forty-eight hours perhaps, I didn't have a sense of consciousness until four or five days later. I was placed in a trauma ward for a week or so. People all around me were dying. A couple of police officers died next to me."

There Is More . . .

It took Scott a full week to be aware of what was going on. Still, he felt calmness around him, a sense that everything would be okay. "I never thought the worst. Even when the doctors told me I would never walk again or do what I used to do, I didn't believe them. I think that was due to God."

The medics put Scott in a trance-like state for the healing process. "They hooked me into a bed that rotated. They stapled my ruptured bladder and collapsed lung. I had lacerations all over my body and a hole in my left cheek. I had cuts and abrasions all down the left side of my body. I also had a broken left foot and a fractured left pelvis.

"After being in the hospital for three weeks, they figured I was stable enough to have my pelvis operation, so I made the decision to have the surgery. It was major. I don't recall much, just a lot of metal screws with a bar across the top that stabilized me, and two screws in the back of my pelvis." Scott smiled. "The doctor held up my x-ray and told me everything went back into place just fine."

Within a month, two female strangers and their significant others came to Scott's bedside and introduced themselves. They were nurses who worked in Los Angeles and had been at Scott's side at the accident. They had witnessed what happened and wanted to share the details with Scott.

"The nurses told me we had a head-on collision. They immediately rushed to help. They found me outside the car and assumed I'd been ejected out the window. One nurse said someone told her to ignore me, saying, 'No vital signs so move on to the next one.' Later they heard me say, 'Please dear God, let me sleep.' That's when one of the nurses dashed toward me.

"They told me that after the accident, there was craziness everywhere. While we lay on the pavement dying, people stole our possessions. The other car in the accident was a Porsche and local people scrambled to pick up valuable items scattered around the cars and injured people. The nurses didn't have time to stop the thieves. They administered first aid and got us out of there.

"My heart was filled with gratitude and joy as one of the nurses told me she rode in my ambulance. She thought she'd die due to the recklessness of the ambulance driver. In another ambulance, my friend, David, was thrown off his gurney, because the driver was driving wild on the side of the road.

"When we arrived at the Tijuana hospital, the American nurses used their own money to purchase items to stabilize us. They insisted that the doctors not operate on us. They wanted to get us to a U.S. hospital for better care. They managed to get us across the border and everyone else went to various hospitals in ambulances. I was airlifted."

Hearing all this, it began to make sense for Scott. I noticed tears in his eyes as he said, "These nurses were my angels. They were sent there at that time, and I'm alive because of it."

Scott stayed at UCSD Medical Center for about six weeks. At first, he didn't have visitors, but as his healing improved, they started to arrive. It was hard for him to socialize because it took so much energy out of him. Most of the time, he just wanted quiet space so he could heal.

The doctors told Scott he couldn't go home unless he showed them he could get in and out of a wheelchair, to and from the toilet, and in and out of bed. "They put me on an elevated thing that brought me up off my bed. I still had a catheter in me and started to use a walker." Scott smiled and told me, "I was continually in a zone of hope, positive wellness, and a place of positive outlook. Nothing ever got me down."

When Scott was released from the hospital, his parents arranged to have a hospital bed set up in their living room. "I felt fortunate to have my parents' assistance because I didn't have a significant other." His parents helped him, yet allowed him to be as independent as possible. The nurses and doctors visited him there. It took about eight months before Scott could walk on his own.

Scott's NDE changed his life. "My near-death experience confirmed there is a Higher Being—God, Buddha, whatever name you choose. I called out to God and here I am today." He smiled broadly. "I see God as electrical energy. Definitely an electrical energy field that can manifest in different realms for everyone.

"There was a period after my NDE when I was clairvoyant. I started to channel messages and heard things about people. It became too much for me. I stopped that ability many years ago. After my NDE, I also saw Spirits—white figures. I couldn't tell if they were male or female. I was in awe at that, and it never scared me."

"I take things more seriously now knowing that, for every cause and effect, there are consequences. We're all intertwined on this plane. We all have an effect on other people. The battle of good and evil, light and dark always goes on. We constantly have those forces around us.

"I'm more loyal and dedicated toward people now, and I expect the same from them and nothing less. Since I've gone to that Light Force and come back, I'm more forgiving and generous. I donate what I can. I help others in my own little way. What lives can I touch? Where am I drawn to help? I follow my instincts.

"I'm more compassionate, loving, and understanding. I feel my emotions deeper than I ever did before. When someone talks about certain people, I feel chills and tingling in my body. It's so profound to watch something and have tears well up in my eyes. I get chills in my body, but it's not frightening. I see it as a confirmation that we're connected. That's life knowing life, reconnecting."

Scott knows it was his desire, will power, and turning to God that kept him alive and gradually got him up walking and surfing again. "You have to maintain hope. You have to know we have the ability within us to make amazing things happen. It's a transcendental state. My healing process took a year or two, however, I never had a negative feeling, like I can't do this, or I won't be able to do this again. I wish I could remember to apply this to everything in my life. It helped my healing process.

"The doctors told my friend who was injured in the accident that he would lose his leg. Hearing those words, he lost the will to move forward. He took it as truth, and his body and brain began to shut down. In his mind, if he lost his leg he would lose his life. It was a painful and long process for him. However, they managed to save his leg."

Scott's advice to others? "When faced with a challenge, go with an open mind and you'll get amazing results."

Like so many people who have had NDEs, Scott hasn't shared his experiences with too many people. "I mentioned the experience to a couple of people and they were surprised. Some thought it was nonsense, hearing information from the spirit

There Is More . . .

realm and seeing Spirits. People have a tendency to judge and get stuck in their beliefs; it's their way or the highway.

Scott is an operations manager at a reproduction graphic company in San Diego. In his free time, he likes to surf, cook, camp in the mountains, ride his bike on the boardwalk, and spend time with his family.

As Scott shared his story with me, it warmed my heart. I could see in his eyes the readiness of his Being longing to speak his truth and expand his awakening. He is ready to follow his heart, surrender his will, and allow Infinite Spirit to guide him.

Scott knew he was too drunk to drive that night in Mexico, and he made the right choice to not slide behind the wheel of a car. However, he was too drunk to realize his friend shouldn't drive as well—a near-fatal mistake.

Thankfully, Spirit angels and Earth angels surround us. Scott's Earth angels appeared at the crash site, nurses from Los Angeles who saved his life out on that road that night. While others stole his possessions, his Earth angel nurses got him emergency care, insisted he be transported to the United States, and paid for his transportation and medical items. Without them, he would never have survived the night.

It was no accident that these nurses arrived when Scott needed emergency help. Coincidences are Divine moments that remind us a Higher Power guides our lives. Scott connected to God when he asked for help, and his Spirit actually assisted the medical team in rolling his body into the emergency room. His Spirit wanted him to live and was highly involved in that process.

When we are healing from trauma or illness, sometimes we need to reserve energy for the process. Though we may appreciate visitors, it consumes a lot of energy, especially when guests want to interact. Out of fear, many visitors chat about meaningless things, afraid of their emotions. If someone does ask you to visit, it is important to speak only from your heart. If a patient asks for privacy, sometimes respecting their healing space is the best gift.

Scott came back with psychic abilities that he used for a while and then began to block. Everyone is capable of tapping into their psychic skills to either bring good to others or use them in a destructive way. In Scott's case, his abilities confirmed that connection. He experienced several miracles, and he continues to inspire others.

Vanessa Chicca
Domestic Violence

"A long time ago at age 16, I found myself married to a fifteen year old, and our daughter was born when I was seventeen," said Vanessa, a quiet, beautiful woman with long silky black hair and dark eyes.

"I was inexperienced and liked being a mom but my husband chafed at this responsibility that had come too soon. There was so much immaturity and so little common sense between the two of us that it makes me cringe today. Four years later, our son was born, but sadly, our marriage ended in divorce before our son's second birthday.

"I had two more children with my second husband, but he was abusive and the abuse escalated. My children and I became more and more afraid."

Tears flooded Vanessa's eyes as she continued. "Unfortunately, that husband took 'till death do us part' too literally and tried to end my life. It was a cool December evening in 1986, and he was very agitated that night. As I put the older children to bed early, fear raced throughout my body. I was holding my tiny nine-week-old daughter in my arms when I told my husband I was going upstairs to put her to bed. He came at me from behind, picked me up by the neck, and choked the life out of me.

"He was six foot six, big guy. I was dangling and embracing my little daughter, and I was trying to claw his hands off my neck." Vanessa paused and looked down. "It didn't work. He had a vice grip on me."

There Is More . . .

For nearly a minute, she breathed hard and tears flowed down her cheeks.

"You can't imagine the terror," she said, pausing again. She found it difficult to continue, then gathered herself.

"The next thing I knew, I wasn't even in my body. The fear, the terror, the pain was all gone. The essence of who I was coursed through the Universe. If you've ever seen Star Trek or Star Wars where stars shoot by—that's what it was like."

Vanessa smiled. "I was really in a hurry. I was just *zooming* and I had this intense sense of freedom, peace, and happiness, like I was headed home. God's Divine Love was calling me back. There are no words to describe how wonderful and happy I felt."

Shortly after, Vanessa heard two sounds almost simultaneously. "One was a horrible moaning sound, which I disregarded. The other was a baby's shrill distress cry. Without a moment's hesitation, I was back in my body. I was making that horrible moaning sound, which again I disregarded, and my tiny nine-week-old daughter was screaming that shrill distress cry."

Vanessa found herself sprawled on the floor across the room from where her husband had picked her up. "I watched him frantically jostle our baby, trying to make her stop crying.

"When I got up off that floor, my knees were knocking and I was shaking, but I was a different person than he had picked up. I was *spiritually empowered*. All of a sudden, I knew I wasn't going to allow domestic violence to be part of my life, and I wasn't afraid to stand up for the rights of myself and my children. What was he going to do, kill me? Been there, done that."

Vanessa convinced her husband to let her take her daughter upstairs. "He was upset, agitated, and didn't want me to take her up, but I convinced him I was just going to put her to bed and I'd be right back down. So he allowed me to go. I tucked my baby in her bassinet, picked up the phone next to her, and called the police."

She wanted to press charges but the official in the DA's office claimed he was "sick and tired of women wasting taxpayers' time and money, only to have them run back to their husbands."

"I told him that wouldn't be the case with me, but he refused to believe I wouldn't, at some point in time, reconcile. With every fiber of my Being, I knew he was wrong.

"I also knew it was one of those turning points forced upon me by powers beyond my control—a power that inflicted inconceivable anguish, a gut-wrenching primal power spawning from feeling desperate to survive and protect my young.

"The official showed me the door, telling me to dry my eyes before leaving. He didn't want anyone to see me crying when I walked out the door. I actually walked out more determined and more empowered.

"It took years and more than one lawyer to help me with the legal battles that followed in the wake of our separation and divorce. My husband once told me he knew I'd come crawling back to him; he was wrong about that, too.

"My children know about my near-death experience, and my youngest is very proud that she called me back, which is why I'm here today." Vanessa laughed. "She reminds me often."

That was the end of Vanessa's near-death experience, but it wasn't the end of the transformation that took place in her life.

There Is More . . .

"Many things changed after my NDE. I became more aware of the life force in every living thing, more aware of nature being a significant part of my life, and how the energy and Light within all of nature shine through me as well. There's a connectedness now—a comfortable connectedness with who I am and of just being me."

It also changed Vanessa's perspective on life. "I'm no longer afraid of death, and I *was* afraid of death before my NDE." She laughed. "I was afraid of *life* before my near-death experience, and now I'm not afraid of life or death.

"This experience brought more joy into my life and I'm a calmer, more centered person. I still get upset. I still have my humanity. But I know what's really important is the purpose I'm here for—to continue to learn, to help my family, and to love others. I'm doing the best I can. When I fulfill my purpose, I'm out of here."

Vanessa is currently serving as chairperson of the San Diego County Coalition for Improving End-of-Life Care. She is also an active member in the San Diego Bereavement Consortium as well as other groups.

Vanessa lives with her third husband, Bob, in Bonita, California. Their beautiful blended family includes three sons, three daughters, and five grandchildren.

In Vanessa's free time, she enjoys writing, painting in watercolors, cooking, gardening, traveling, and spending time with her family. She is the author of *Love Is Your Legacy, The Teeny Tiny Diet Book,* and *Create Your Own Cookbook Kit.*

Vanessa Chicca

My heart and soul ached for Vanessa and her children when she described their violent home life. What a blessing that she not only survived but is now living a thriving life with passion and a sense of Oneness. God is her guiding Light.

Like so many women who live in domestic violence, Vanessa was caught between responsibility for her children and her instinct to leave her husband. At the time, society considered it important to keep the family together regardless of the quality of life.

If you're in a situation that doesn't lift you up, leap out in faith and know Infinite Spirit will be there to guide and protect you.

If a man or woman abuses you once, it's only a matter of time before it happens again. What would it take for you to leave an abusive relationship?

When faced with her death, Vanessa realized that a powerful force within her could overcome anything, and it was important for her to protect her children as well as herself. She didn't know how she would survive financially, but she trusted in God because she knew she was doing the right thing by pressing charges against her husband.

Have faith that every circumstance you encounter and every person you meet has a purpose—to further your growth. Be willing to let go of that which no longer serves you, even if change is frightening. Staying stuck is not living.

Tianna Conte, PhD
Heat-Induced Heart Failure

Since the late 1970s, Tianna has had a private practice as a psycho-spiritual therapist specializing in enlightened self-care and personal evolution. She still assists clients in transforming adversities into triumphs that enhance their lives.

After her near-death experience in June 1995, however, she could not practice the same way. Her NDE taught her there's a gift in every pain. The key is not lingering in the pain but moving through it as soon as possible to feel powerful in the here and now.

In 1995, Tianna was prompted to go to a spa in Manhattan for a full body wrap. Not quite where you'd expect to experience an NDE . . .

"My 'mummy wrap' consisted of eighteen rolls of ace bandages wrapped around every limb and a vinyl suit covering the trunk of my body. Once I lay down, eight blankets covered me and a blindfold shielded my eyes. The experience was designed to detoxify my body of stress."

She called the treatment "a little anxiety-provoking," then she noticed her heart beating rapidly. Trained as a physician, she knew it was arrhythmic, as her heart was beating too fast. Yet she didn't focus on it.

"Then the heat became more intense, the heartbeat more intense, and the next thing, LIGHT. Pure, radiant, blue-white Light, like from a glacier." She felt one with that Light.

There Is More . . .

"The Light was free and I felt free. Every cell of the non-existent me was bathed in that white Light filled with love. I was just hanging out in the Light when I heard, *It's not your time to cross over.*"

Puzzled, she thought, *Cross over what?*

She was feeling free and expansive with Beings silently talking to her. Telepathically, she asked them why she was there and was told, *To have an experience to pass on to others.*

"They told me birth and death are the same. Birth is celebrated because it's known and death feared because it's unknown, but it's all about Oneness. One is coming into form and one is leaving form behind after having an adventure called life."

As she shared her story, Tianna smiled and said she wished she could have taken notes, the communication was so good.

"I felt like I was All, but how could that be? I was part of the All because I had no body or senses that separated me."

The Beings went on to tell Tianna, *The ego and the illusion of the senses block this knowing. The portals of agony and ecstasy allow us to transcend the everyday world and see the deeper picture, the connection to All.*

"Then the Beings went on to share this: *In every moment there is a choice, but it doesn't matter what choice you make—whether it is aligned to your spiritual structure or reactive to the ego—the experience of the journey will be different, but the end result will be the same.*"

Then Tianna was sucked back into her body. A body wrap that was supposed to be twenty minutes had lasted an hour and a half—the spa attendants had forgotten her! "Landing under all the bandages and blankets had gone beyond hot and outrageous and *PAINFUL*. It felt almost like the layers of conditioning that suppress us."

Then she realized she had freed her body. "Don't ask me how, but somehow my hands were above the blankets and I was ripping them off when the attendant remembered me."

She didn't know at the time she had a near-death experience. "I thought it was the most ultimate de-stresser, detoxifier I ever experienced! I was so light I could barely stand. I felt tingly." All her senses were heightened. "Everything was vivid. I was in bliss."

She enjoyed the experience so much that she kept going to spas for body wraps, hoping to revisit the experience!

Tianna called it a "near-death-like experience," and it wasn't until she talked to her husband and doctors years later that they said, "Your heart stopped—you should know that." Her husband understood her and wanted to hear about her experience, which made it easier to integrate the NDE into her life.

Since Tianna's near-death experience, everything has changed. She said, "Perception can never be the same after an NDE. I have no fear of death, but a deep faith in life." She mentioned that the thing she'd wanted most in life—inner peace, the ability to hear that still small voice inside—came as a gift from her NDE.

"I hear that small tiny voice as the main voice, and I'm so humbled by that."

She knows now what she suspected all along—that we shouldn't compare ourselves to the Light because we *ARE* the Light.

There Is More . . .

"I was told to pass this message on to others. Now I realize the message is to support others in the awareness that we are amazing Spiritual Beings, greater than what our limited minds and senses perceive."

She asks, "If I am and we are one with Light, with Love, and with possibilities, how come we're playing so limited?"

Tianna believes that completing her projects is why she returned from the Light. That includes her books, *Love's Fire: Beyond Mortal Boundaries* and *Love's Fire: Living the Awakened Journey;* her upcoming documentary *Awaken Your Riches*; and her innovative work in applying quantum physics to shift limiting beliefs without conscious effort. You can contact Tianna through her e-mail at tiannacd@gmail.com.

Tianna has been a joy to get to know. Every five minutes, she had me laughing and I know how healing laughter is to the body, mind, and Spirit.

Trained as a physician, Tianna was so into the experience of her NDE that she didn't realize she had died. Instead, she was wrapped in pure bliss, support, love, and Light.

How often do you find yourself so present with something or someone that time escapes you? The present moment is the only place to be.

Tianna shows that you can receive wisdom from the spirit realm and that life is about heart, not ego. Open yourself up to receive that which is for your highest good in Divine law and order. Trust that when you seek, you will find.

✧ ✧ ✧
The Common Thread

In these stories, beautiful people, young and old, present a common thread. They all speak about love for life, connection to Spirit, and a spiritual awakening to who they truly are—Spiritual Beings. They feel connected to the source of life, Creation. This expression can now be part of all they do and say.

Before their NDEs, they had limited views of life; now they see themselves as part of the Divine expression of life.

As a child, I used to think that the closer I sat up front in church near the priest, the closer I was to God. A lot of people believe they need to attend church to be close to Infinite Spirit, or that God and spirituality is something outside of them.

What I've learned through NDEs is that God is within us. We ARE the Light, and we are all connected to everyone and everything. If Infinite Spirit is within us, isn't God with us at all times? All we need to do is silence the chatter of the mind and tap into the small voice within to hear the truth. There is no separation except in our minds.

After their NDEs or out-of-body experiences, all the people we interviewed experienced a profound sense of peace, immense love, and calmness. Those who had been ill felt healed. They also felt the oneness of all, communicated with the spirit realm, and many noticed sensory changes when they came back into their bodies. They felt reborn. Time shifted for many, with no sense of time when they were outside their bodies.

Experiences in the tunnel of Light vary. Some people see or feel brightness, others darkness, still others see bright colors.

Movement varies as well; some people tumble through the tunnel, others move slowly, and some even feel as if they were sucked through a vacuum or fell down a slide. People sometimes hear things, such as voices, wind, or music, while other's experience silence in the tunnel.

Tianna explained how many of these changes can be explained by the experience of Oneness, "I had no body or senses that separated me." When someone has no boundaries that separate them from Love and Light, they feel connected and whole. With no limiting senses, colors are brighter, vision is sharper, and Spirits easily communicated telepathically.

Once NDErs return to their bodies, some of these characteristics remain, sometimes for a brief period, other times long term. Life is precious, and several of them said, "I was just happy to be alive!" Circumstances don't take precedent, the Heart and Divine Love rule their lives.

With their fears about dying alleviated, many now entertain a new belief system that aligns with their truth. They appreciate life, their places in it, value others more, are less judgmental and more compassionate.

After our NDEs, we understand at a deeper heart level that the veil between life and death is thin and each breath of life is precious and sacred. We are not our bodies; we are Spiritual Beings here to learn, to love, to grow, to embrace the Oneness of All, to discover and reclaim the sacred connection within us.

People shared their experiences of near-death, coming from a place of fear, of lack—a three-dimensional perception. In an instant, they expanded their awareness to include the Universe, beyond the stars. In letting go, they surrendered and detached from the three-dimensional reality they think they're in. Most found everything they ever wished for and more.

Maybe that ability is already in us. If we can allow ourselves to let go, even for a split second, we can touch that reality.

At birth, we enter a society that tells us how to look, how to behave, and what to think. Sometimes people are thrown into situations like near-death experiences where they are blasted out of that material reality and into another level. Most of us wonder how we can access some of that knowledge, how to experience something that can take us beyond our daily lives without having to nearly die.

I believe we can achieve this by effectively using meditation, prayer, or yoga to calm and center ourselves. Another effective method is spending time in nature; it's available to all of us, and it's free. Take time to watch the sunrise, sit on the beach or next to a pond, or walk under the trees. Some people like to play with their pets, listen to music, or hold a baby. All of these can help us access more of who we truly are inside, connecting us to the big picture of life.

Life is a process, a constant flow of change. It's why we're on the planet, and when our current cycle is complete, regardless of human-created time, we move on. Death is not an ending but a beginning to life anew in another realm, where we immediately heal from the wounds and worries of this lifetime and transform to bathe in loving Light, bliss and peace.

As humans, most of what we fear will never come to pass. In between fear and wishes, we live one day at a time, filling our moments with the life we choose, where our thoughts lead us. Unexpected things happen, but if we can practice acceptance, appreciation, deal with the current moment, feel the emotions, and move forward, we can remain happy and content, despite our expectations and frustrations.

Life is change. Invite change into your life for your highest good.

The stories in this book highlight the idea that living in the moment is our only true life. Emotions that take us out of the moment and throw us into worries about the future or regrets about the past are a waste of time. Learn from the moment, live in the moment. It's what we were born to do.

These stories also highlight the importance of accepting others and their stages of life experience. No one is perfect. We are all here to learn and to grow. We are perfect in our current state because we are made in the image of Infinite Spirit.

However, if someone is destructive, of course it's wise to move from that energy. It's not uncommon for people to have destructive thoughts and behaviors. We can learn from these people, step away from them, and stand in our truth—Love. Perhaps these examples of living in love can help other people witness our actions.

Stress pushes us to change. Anger at God moves us to a new place. Every challenge contains a gift, and if we're willing to explore that possibility, every challenge can offer blessings.

We're all here to learn, to grow, and help others along the way. My desire is that this book has helped you, and you will share this wisdom with others so their paths can be clear of fears blocking their way.

Always remember who you are—Light, and Love. Celebrate your life and its gift to the world.

Love and Blessings,

Sharon

Sharon

✧ ✧ ✧
Heartfelt Love and Appreciation

Nikki, Bernie, Tessa, Dominique, Colter, Nancy, John, Alexis, Jil, Dan, Carla, Helen, Scott, Vanessa, and Tianna, I truly felt blessed and honored to be able to interview you for *There Is More . . . 18 Near-Death Experiences.*

My heart and soul was filled with joy and love as you openly shared your experiences and wisdom with me. I know for some of you, your NDE actually became a healing process and allowed you to embrace life on a deeper and more heartfelt level.

Through your stories, you have captured the essence of who we truly are and shown that we are all connected in LOVE!

I send you love and blessings as you continue your journey. You bring into the world Light and Love!

P.M.H. Atwater, Michael Bernard Beckwith, Larry Dossey, Stephen and Ondrea Levine, Jeffrey and Jody Long, and LaVon Switzer, my heart is filled with deep gratitude and love. Thank you for your endorsements and support for our book.

I know each of you in your own way makes a profound difference in people's lives. You share your wisdom with truth, compassion, and love. You see the big picture in life and assist others to broaden their horizons. P.M.H., Michael, Larry, Stephen, Ondrea, Jeffrey, Jody, and LaVon, you are bright beacons of light, making the road easier for people to find their way. Thank you for being in my life. I'm blessed and honored to know you.

There Is More . . .

Miko Radcliffe and Jeaneen Lund, your creativity and eye have been blessings to us in many projects. We love you and appreciate you on many levels.

✧ ✧ ✧

My Amazing Project Team

In the past five years, everything I created has been Divinely guided from Infinite Spirit. I feel heartfelt appreciation for being open to service.

As we travel through life, we are blessed to meet special people and I consider Monica Hagen one of mine. She's my Earth angel.

Monica came into my life in 2007 when she asked me to present a workshop at her Dragonfly Art Center. The moment we met, we knew there was a deep connection—from the past to the future—and we quickly became friends and then business partners.

Monica edited my books and we worked together on our documentary, *Dying to Live: NDE* and *Mustang Man: How a Wild Horse Tamed a Vietnam Vet*. We found that when we set our intention and committed to a project, it was Divinely guided and everything and everyone came about with ease and grace.

Infinite Spirit brought Hector into my life to heal my past and amplify my heart to give and receive love in a boundless way. He has been my strength through all the projects. His questions and wisdom brought forth deeper messages and richer finished products.

After we created the two documentaries, Monica, Hector, and I were Divinely guided to move forward with the next project, which you now hold in your hands—true stories from men, women, and children about their near-death experiences.

There Is More . . .

My heart and Spirit is expansive because of the love, support, understanding, vision, and teamwork Monica, Hector, and I have with one another and Infinite Spirit on our projects. We're now open to Divine guidance for our next one.

Appendix

✧ ✧ ✧
Frequently Asked Questions

When we screen our documentary, *Dying to LIVE: NDE*, Monica, Hector, and I invite people to ask us questions. Below are some of the frequently asked questions and our responses.

How do you explain your miraculous healing?

My healing started when my daughter, Jeaneen, entered my hospital room. My entire Being lit up when I saw her, and she ran to me and crawled into my bed and cradled me in her arms. That's when I truly believe my miraculous healing began. Nothing could hold me back—I had seen and connected with my daughter.

After being with Jeaneen, I felt the freedom of my Spirit not being attached to anything physical. I was free from the world of structure that was holding me back.

Being in the Light and Love of Infinite Spirit and feeling the Light within every cell of my Being reminded me that, at my core level, the Light of God is within me and everyone.

My healing ultimately came from Infinite Spirit, and I returned to the planet to share that message.

Why do some people have an NDE while others die?

I really don't know the answer. Perhaps some people have completed this lifetime here on Earth, while others still have contributions that are vital.

As humans on the planet, we don't understand the "Big Picture," we have to keep faith that things work out as they should, even if

There Is More . . .

we don't like it. A life as short as that of a stillborn child affects the world, whether it's the parents, family members, or perhaps a nurse. It's not about quantity of life, but quality. Life is so much more complex than we realize, and it's not up to us to judge what is an early death. It's how we deal with the world that matters, so love one another and treat everyone well, including yourself.

Why are some people given a choice to return and others forced to come back?

We are all individuals and each experience is unique. Some people telepathically hear the voice of Infinite Spirit and are given an option to return, such as with me. Other people are told they have to return for a loved one, or they have more lessons to learn. Some people just wake up from their NDE.

I believe some people are given the choice to return because life is not arbitrary but a gift. If those given the choice have experienced enough love on the planet, they would choose to stay in the spirit realm. If their love for someone on Earth includes unfinished business, they might choose to return to their physical bodies. I believe the choice is always about love.

Also, perhaps they have learned most of their lessons and don't need to return to expand their journey at that time. However, if they decide to return to their Earthly body, their life will be on a path of deeper expression and love.

For those who don't have a choice but are sent back, this experience usually makes the person extremely angry, but there is a higher purpose for their return. Sometimes we may never know that purpose, but the impact of an NDE can be far reaching.

Is it hard to adjust back into the body after an NDE?

It's common to hear people who have had an NDE say they have a hard time adjusting to being back in their bodies. When they were in Spirit, they felt no boundaries, just freedom. Also, they experienced themselves as energy instead of material mass.

I didn't have a difficult time adjusting back into my body, maybe because my life force was so low and I was brought back to life cell by cell. My body had time to adjust as it was being healed. I felt fortunate and blessed by my experience on many levels.

Why do people have a hard time being back on the planet after an NDE?

There are so many reasons.

It's difficult for a lot of people when they come back to the Earth plane because in their daily lives they experience frustration and a lot of mixed emotions. They also miss the immense love, freedom, joy, and peace they felt when out of their physical bodies.

Sometimes NDErs feel as if a part of them is caught between the two realms, and they don't feel that their physical body is integrated with the Light.

Some people's NDEs weren't as expansive as mine. My Spirit was lifted out of my body and I went through my life review, the tunnel, into the Light, relived events, and my life changed forever. However, it's important to mention it's not about the number of steps; it's about the impact and aftereffects that matter.

A lot of people in our society don't understand what we experienced. They think we're crazy or have made up the event.

There Is More . . .

Some NDErs can't find the support they need and desire, and that's extremely hard on them. To find a group near you, as well as valuable information, go to IANDS.org.

Some people aren't living their life purposes and are tired of their mundane lives. In reality, we can create any life we choose.

I also believe some people who long to be in the Light have forgotten they ARE the Light and never separate from it.

When you leave your physical body, you leave behind the material world and discover what is really important—LOVE!

How was life different after your NDE?

After my NDE, I realized I am an extension of God's love. I have integrated my experience by fully expressing my truth and sharing my expression of love with others. I no longer proclaim to do things "my way"; I go within and seek Divine guidance as a way of life, which allows people, events, and things for my highest good to flow to me and through me with ease and grace. I invite Infinite Spirit to move through me.

Also, my life is different since my NDE because I am living my life purpose with passion and love. I am still not perfect, but I live knowing that I am headed in the right direction, in love.

What changes remain and which go back to normal after an NDE?

Everyone is different, so what happens when they return to their physical bodies after an NDE would be different. Some people come back with heightened senses of colors, sounds, smells, touch, sight, and new awarenesses, and the changes may stay with them for a short time or a long time.

Frequently Asked Questions

Some people who come back with psychic abilities lose them before long, while other people allow their abilities to assist them and others—even as a profession.

Regarding spirit guides or angels in the spirit realm, the people whom I have met who experienced them still hold the spirit guides and angels close to their hearts and minds. Perhaps they communicate with them through meditation or other means. These people understand they are not alone and the spirit guides and angels are here to assist us when we call upon them.

The ultimate lasting change is Love, Oneness of All, and the preciousness of each breath of life.

What is the message of an NDE?

Some people receive messages just for them, and others receive messages to share with humanity. However, after a near-death experience, most of the people I know agree the main messages are:

- There's only Love, a Universal unconditional Love.

- There is no separation; we are connected in Oneness and Love.

- God is within.

- Life is a precious gift from Infinite Spirit. Stop taking life for granted.

- Death is not our enemy, it is merely a doorway.

- We are not our bodies. We are souls residing in a physical body while on this Earth plane.

- Don't fear death because it's the ultimate freedom. You never die—your Spirit lives on forever.

- The Light is brighter than you think and more powerful than you imagine. This powerful bright Light is in the center of our Being, which we can tap into at any moment.

- Time and space, as we know it, does not exist on the other side and it feels like a state of never-ending love.

- Love unconditionally, forgive ourselves and others, and grow in awareness.

- NDEs are powerful and they can be life changing, even a distressed NDE.

Do you think people who die experience the same things as NDEers?

We don't know for sure. However, I believe each person who makes their transition does experience some of the same things, such as being greeted by someone, shown a review of his or her life, or traveling through the tunnel of Light. Then it's up to their beliefs if they see a spiritual being like Jesus, Buddha, Krishna, the Virgin Mary, Kwan Yin, a relative or friend, or perhaps a special pet.

I believe, no matter the outcome, the person who dies will become united in immense Love and Light. If the person made their transition due to illness, from my experience, they would immediately feel healed upon leaving their physical body.

What do you think happens after the tunnel?

Wow. My heart is pounding. I wish I knew. All I can say is it has to be magnificent being in the pure Light, immense love, and freedom. When I close my eyes and ask the question, I see a radiant glow. I hope I gain a lot more wisdom when I make my transition.

Perhaps true life comes as we remember we are Love and Light.

Explain emotions of bliss, love, healing, acceptance, life review, and reliving.

I can't describe the bliss because it's beyond words, it is a feeling we can't describe.

When my Spirit lifted out of my body and hovered above it, I no longer felt pain, weakness, nausea, or sickness. I felt healthy, pain free, vibrant, energized, and more alive than ever before.

When I let go of my physical body, my Spirit soared. The love I felt was beyond anything I experienced here. The closest feeling I felt here on this Earth plane is the love I have for my daughter, but it was multiplied beyond numbers. You can't even begin to comprehend the love felt in the spirit realm in the Light of God.

Witnessing the review of my life, I felt humbled and honored to see the difference I had made in some people's lives. When I relived some times with my beautiful daughter Jeaneen, I actually cried at the joy of being pregnant with her and giving birth. I was reliving precious moments. I could feel the measureless love between us and the profound difference we made in each other's lives, and to other people. Jeaneen taught me about true love. It was a blessing to not just recall or see our lives together, but RELIVE them!

Jeaneen's love is the reason I returned to continue my life.

If being dead is so wonderful, why would anyone want to return to the planet?

To clarify, I believe we don't die, our souls live on.

Most of the people I met who have had NDEs came back because they saw a loved one or heard their voice. The love for the person or people brought them back into the attached Earthly plane.

During an NDE, many people learn more about who they are and why their lifetime is important. In seeing more of the "Big Picture," the value of each life can grow. Many can't wait to get back to the planet, to share that knowledge and start living their life purpose.

Some people rediscover a deeper, more meaningful love, beyond anything they could have imagined.

Life on the planet is temporary, so why not open up and embrace our experience here as one aspect of the whole?

Explain the heightened senses.

After an NDE, experiencers often notice that smells might be stronger, colors appear brighter, objects look sharper (like they are in 3D), and they might have increased sensitivity to touch. Their sight may include seeing Beings from other realms. They may have increased psychic abilities and find it easy to communicate with those in the spirit realm.

For some people their heightened senses may last a short time and for others it may linger throughout their lives.

Frequently Asked Questions

Explain the colors on the other side.

Wow. The colors are alive, vibrant, radiant, energized, soothing, warm, and loving. Being in the Light of God is beyond any words we have in our vocabulary. It's absolutely magnificent. The closest thing I have seen here on this Earth plane is the aurora borealis (Northern Lights), but nothing comes close to comparing the Light of Infinite Spirit.

Explain the use of telepathy on the other side.

Communication in the spirit realms is free and effortless. No words are spoken, yet all is heard. It's effortless because it's based on love, freedom, and oneness, not on worries or fears. This communication is a vibration. It is effortless because it has no contradiction, it's easy because it has no attachments. The telepathic communication is beautiful because it's free and alive. Telepathy is the quiet voice of expression.

Explain the sense of oneness you can access once you return from an NDE.

An NDE reminds a person they are connected to the oneness of everyone and everything. Some people realize this without having to experience an NDE. Everything is vibration and therefore connected and united in the oneness of ALL.

Once a person understands this at the core of their Being, their life transforms. They treat people with respect, dignity, and love, they respect nature, they feel gratitude for what they have. They see and honor the Divinity in everything and everyone.

When people realize and embrace the Oneness, racism and discrimination will disappear, and illness will decrease since much chronic stress is brought on by our fears.

Why would someone have an unpleasant NDE?

Not long ago, there wasn't a lot of research about distressed NDEs. Now we know that about 1% to 15% of NDEs are distressing. During their distressed NDE, people may experience emotionally-painful feelings such as fear, horror, terror, anger, loneliness, isolation, and/or guilt.

Perhaps people have distressed NDEs because of unresolved, painful emotions in their lives. What I learned is that the people who have unpleasant NDEs usually realize they have to change some behavior or belief, and the distressed NDE assists them to get back on track.

Do you believe there's a Hell?

I believe Hell is not a place but a state of mind. You make Hell your reality by what you think and do.

I've learned from distressed NDEs that our fear is our Hell. There is always Light available to us if we look for it—go to the Light. Living in fear is living in Hell, right here on Earth.

Is there a Heaven?

It depends on who you ask. Christians believe Heaven is a place in the sky.

Can Heaven be a state of mind?

Many times throughout the day, I experience Heaven. There are times I am attuned and absorbed within the perfection of the Oneness of All, with the presence of Infinite Spirit all around me. A deep sense of inner peace, joy, tranquility, and love radiates around and through me.

We are all Heavenly Beings. If God is within us and there is no separation, isn't Heaven within us? When you quiet yourself, the voice comes from within, not from above.

I believe when we make our transitions, our Spirits move into another realm. Some people would call this Heaven. I'm not sure what I would name it. All I know is when I visited the spirit realm, I was more alive than ever before, and I loved the feeling and sensation of where I was.

What is God?

It depends on who you ask. Some people believe God to be a human image, a Heavenly Father looking down on us from his throne in the clouds. Others believe God to be all loving or judgmental. Some people don't even use the word God, they use Buddha, Great Spirit, Creator, Tao, Yahweh, Allah, Higher Power and hundreds of other names. Some people consider God to be female, therefore Goddess.

I believe God is pure love and energy and not form. To me, God is everything that moves through everyone, ever present all the time, and we are an expression of God. I believe God/Infinite Spirit is limitless, therefore, why would God limit himself or herself to a single image or gender?

Explain about spirit guides' and angels' roles in an NDE.

We all have spirit guides and angels to assist us in all our spiritual experiences. In an NDE, they appear as loving greeters or reviewers who assist you in the review of your life, and they may lead you to the tunnel, somewhere else, toward a loved one, or into the Light.

While on Earth we can tap into our angels and spirits guides for support, love, and guidance. They can't interfere with your life, so you have to ask for their assistance.

How can we feel Oneness without having to die or have an NDE?

You can connect to the feeling of an NDE through your breath, meditation, feeling freedom, seeing beauty, living in the moment, through love, and by speaking your truth.

Quiet time is a great way to connect to the big picture, to Oneness with all realms. Spending time alone in nature is a great way to connect, as is watching a baby or animal. Most cats are in the present moment most of the time. See how they love the feel of the carpet on their feet, the stroke of a loving owner's hand, the cold tickle of water that makes them shake their paws. Dogs love unconditionally. Birds connect to their flock and respond as one. Fish breathe their environment. We can learn a lot by just observing and then practicing what we see.

Being in the moment is key.

Can we communicate with people who have died?

When my loving brother Tommy made his transition, he came to me for eighteen years in my dreams, which were more real than real life. He also appeared before me when I was awake and alert. Tommy seemed to be physical, yet he wasn't—I could see through him.

My mom made her transition years ago and she first appeared to me as a Spirit I could see through, like Tommy. She looked healthy, vibrant, energized, and full of love. She would talk to me and sometimes give me messages for Jeaneen or my sister,

Joyce. Now she turns on the water or flicks the lights off and on three times when she wants my attention.

When a person first makes their transition, I believe they are close to the Earth plane for some time and if you are open, you have an opportunity to connect with them. Remember, the veil between life and death is thin.

If you're not able to see the person, perhaps you'll feel their presence around you, or notice a scent that reminds you of them (pipe smoke, perfume or flowers), or feel a brush or kiss upon your face. Be open-minded and aware of the signs that come your way. It might be your loved one getting your attention—even if only to let you know they are fine.

In meditation and prayer, we can communicate with them. Some people get specific information, some get comfort or a feeling of connectedness. We can all communicate on multiple levels. The more we practice, the better we get at the skill. Prayer is talking to the other realms, meditation is listening.

What happens in a violent death?

I believe when a person has a violent death, their Spirit is lifted out of the physical body prior to the violence so he or she never experiences the pain.

What do you think happens to a person who takes their own life?

When a person takes their life, they think they end their current suffering and pain, but I believe they will have to come back and repeat the same lessons they were trying to avoid. Better to face up to our problems and deal with them directly rather than put them off and perhaps intensify them. Often, people commit suicide over situations that are temporary, and if they could see the big picture, they might shift their perspectives. Each challenge contains a gift—are you ready to accept your gift?

When people die, do they all go to the peaceful place you talk about?
In Dr. Eric Pearl's book, *The Reconnection: Heal Others, Heal Yourself*, he shares his mother's NDE where she went through three different levels. Some people have experienced the same levels, others have different experiences. As individuals, we may experience something as simple as driving to the store from totally different points of view. It makes sense that our NDEs would have variety as well.

Does everyone see their dead relatives during an NDE?

Some people do see a loved one during their NDE. However, not everyone sees a loved one who has died before them.

NDEs aren't about seeing anyone. I believe the purpose of the NDE is for the person to reconnect with their Being, and unconditional love.

Do people see what they expect when they die, like Pearly Gates, God, etc.?

No one knows for sure. Maybe it's best to say we see whatever we need to see.

If people believe in Pearly Gates, then that's probably what they will see. In the interviews, John saw a blue crystal cave because, in his Native American studies with his grandmother, that was his experience. Since then, he has retained his connection to crystals. Carla saw angels because of her belief in angels. I believe that whatever a person believes is what they will see and who they will see, including animals. It makes sense that what comforts us will be shown during the transition.

I know from my NDE experience that everyone eventually will see and become one with the Light.

What's happening to a person when they are dying and say they see someone? Are they hallucinating?

From my experience being around people as they prepare to make their transitions, the person is actually going in and out of both the physical realm and the spirit realm. What they see is real. Many are not hallucinating from medications. When they say something like, "I see Dad," or grandma, angels, their favorite pet, etc., they are not making it up. You might want to ask the dying person what they hear and what else they see. Ask questions and get as many details as you can before they make their transition. You can learn a lot from them and your interactions may help bring them comfort.

Did your ex-husband ever admit to you he was infected with AIDS?

Yes, Bill called me a few weeks before he made his transition and admitted he was infected with AIDS when he married me in 1983, and it was him on the Dan Rather's AIDS special. He also told me he led a secret bi-sexual lifestyle, before, during and after our marriage.

Were you able to forgive him for infecting you?

Yes, decades ago I forgave Bill and also my grandfather for their behaviors and actions. As long as I didn't forgive them, they had a hold on my life and well-being, and any anger I held onto would destroy my immune system. I realized forgiveness is for me and no one else, and through forgiveness I was able to reclaim my power and dignity.

Forgiveness doesn't mean accepting the behavior, it just releases the burden, the energy attached to the anger, leaving the mind, body and Spirit free to invest energy into other places in our lives.

When did you tell your parents about being raped as a child?

I didn't tell my parents about my grandfather until I was in the hospital being treated for anorexia. The doctor told me I wouldn't heal until the truth came out. I remember I called my parents and when my dad heard what his father did to me for nine years, with rage in his voice he told me, "I'd kill him today if he were still alive."

Why do you think you had to go through so much trauma in your life, such as sexual abuse, bad relationships, suicide attempts, and HIV/AIDS?

This may be hard for some people to understand, but I believe that before we are born we choose our lessons. I chose ALL my experiences—my parents, abuse, illnesses, relationships—so I would open up my heart and grow in love and forgiveness.

Each and every challenge I faced was a blessing because it brought me to self-discovery, wholeness, love, and living my life purpose with passion.

Any final thoughts?

It is an honor and a blessing to be able to share my experiences with you and to be walking upon Mother Earth. Please remember that you are the Light. You are the Divinity. You are One with everyone and everything. You are LOVED!

✧ ✧ ✧
Verifying a Near-Death Experience

We would like to thank Dr. Bruce Greyson for permission to share this scale used to verify a Near-Death Experience for research purposes.

1. Did time seem to speed up or slow down?
0 = No
1 = Time seemed to go faster or slower than usual
2 = Everything seemed to be happening at once; or time stopped or lost all meaning

2. Were your thoughts speeded up?
0 = No
1 = Faster than usual
2 = Incredibly fast

3. Did scenes from your past come back to you?
0 = No
1 = I remembered many past events
2 = My past flashed before me, out of my control

4. Did you suddenly seem to understand everything?
0 = No
1 = Everything about myself or others
2 = Everything about the Universe

5. Did you have a feeling of peace or pleasantness?
0 = No
1 = Relief or calmness
2 = Incredible peace or pleasantness

6. Did you have a feeling of joy?
0 = No
1 = Happiness
2 = Incredible joy

7. Did you feel a sense of harmony or unity with the Universe?
0 = No
1 = I felt no longer in conflict with nature
2 = I felt united or one with the world

8. Did you see, or feel surrounded by, a brilliant light?
0 = No
1 = An unusually bright light
2 = A light clearly of mystical or other-worldly origin

9. Were your senses more vivid than usual?
0 = No
1 = More vivid than usual
2 = Incredibly more vivid

10. Did you seem to be aware of things going on elsewhere, as if by extrasensory perception (ESP)?
0 = No
1 = Yes, but the facts have not been checked out
2 = Yes, and the facts have been checked out

11. Did scenes from the future come to you?
0 = No
1 = Scenes from my personal future
2 = Scenes from the world's future

12. Did you feel separated from your body?
0 = No
1 = I lost awareness of my body
2 = I clearly left my body and existed outside it

13. Did you seem to enter some other, unearthly world?
0 = No
1 = Some unfamiliar and strange place
2 = A clearly mystical or unearthly realm

14. Did you seem to encounter a mystical being or presence, or hear an unidentifiable voice?
0 = No
1 = I heard a voice I could not identify
2 = I encountered a definite being, or a voice clearly of mystical or unearthly origin

15. Did you see deceased or religious Spirits?
0 = No
1 = I sensed their presence
2 = I actually saw them

16. Did you come to a border or point of no return?
0 = No
1 = I came to a definite conscious decision to "return" to life
2 = I came to a barrier that I was not permitted to cross; or was "sent back" against my will

SCORING
A score of 7 or higher is considered an NDE for research purposes. The main score among a large sample of near-death experiences is 15.

I want to thank IANDS, International Association of Near-Death Studies, at iands.org, for allowing me to share the next ten pages of valuable information from their website.

✧ ✧ ✧
Definitions of an NDE, OBE, and dNDE

What is a Near-Death Experience (NDE)?

A near-death experience, or NDE, is a profound psychological event that may occur to a person close to death or who is not near death but in a situation of physical or emotional crisis. Being in a life-threatening situation does not, by itself, constitute a near-death experience. It is the pattern of perceptions, creating a recognizable overall event, that has been called "near-death experience."

An NDE typically includes a sense of moving, often at great speed and usually through a dark space, into a fantastic landscape and encountering beings that may be perceived as sacred figures, deceased family members or friends, or unknown entities. A pinpoint of indescribable light may grow to surround the person in brilliant but not painful radiance; unlike physical light, it is not merely visual but is sensed as being an all-loving presence that many people define as the Supreme Being of their religious faith.

What is an Out-of-Body-Experience (OBE)?

An NDE may begin with an out-of-body experience (OBE)—a very clear perception of being somehow separate from one's physical body, possibly even hovering nearby and watching events going on around the body.

What is a Distressing Near-Death Experience (dNDE)?

Most near-death experiencers (NDErs) report that their experience was dominated by pleasurable feelings such as peace, joy, and bliss. However, less commonly, some NDErs have reported that their experience was dominated by distressing, emotionally-painful feelings such as fear, terror, horror, anger, loneliness, isolation, and/or guilt.

After a disturbing NDE, a person will almost always look for an explanation for having had the experience; because many interpret it as a threat or warning, they may try to change habits or behaviors, or take up a new religious practice, hoping to avoid a recurrence. However, as experiencers adjust to these personal transformations, they often have difficulty finding someone they trust to tell about the event. They usually feel in great need of information and support.

✧ ✧ ✧
Characteristics of a Near-Death Experience

Most NDEs are felt as peaceful and loving, but some are disturbing. Each near-death experience is unique, but as a group NDEs display common features.

- Intense emotions: commonly of profound peace, well-being, love; others marked by fear, horror, loss
- A perception of seeing one's body from above (called an out-of-body experience or OBE), sometimes watching medical resuscitation efforts or moving instantaneously to other places
- Rapid movement through darkness, often toward an indescribable light
- A sense of being "somewhere else" in a landscape that may seem like a spiritual realm or world
- Incredibly rapid, sharp thinking and observations
- Encounter with deceased loved ones, possibly sacred figures (the Judges, Jesus, a saint) or unrecognized beings, with whom communication is mind-to-mind; these figures may seem consoling, loving, or terrifying
- A life review, reliving actions and feeling their emotional impact on others
- In some cases, a flood of knowledge about life and the nature of the planet
- Sometimes a decision to return to the body
- The same elements appear in both pleasant and distressing near-death experiences, but with different emotional tones

Characteristics of a Near-Death Experience

P.M.H. Atwater, one of the most prolific NDE researchers, in her book *Coming Back to Life*, described a peaceful experience this way:

- A sensation of floating out of one's body. Often followed by an out-of-body experience where all that goes on around the "vacated" body is both seen and heard accurately.
- Passing through a dark tunnel or black hole or encountering some kind of darkness. This is often accompanied by a feeling or sensation of movement or acceleration. "Wind" may be heard or felt.
- Ascending toward a light at the end of the darkness. A light of incredible brilliance, with the possibility of seeing people, animals, plants, lush outdoors, and even cities within the light.
- Greeted by friendly voices, people or beings who may be strangers, loved ones, or religious figures. Conversation can ensue, information or a message may be given.
- Seeing a panoramic review of the life just lived, from birth to death or in reverse order, sometimes becoming a reliving of the life rather than a dispassionate viewing. The person's life can be reviewed in its entirety or in segments. This is usually accompanied by a feeling or need to assess loss or gains during the life to determine what was learned or not learned. Other beings can take part in this judgment-like process or offer advice.
- A reluctance to return to the Earth plane, but invariably realizing either their job on Earth is not finished or a mission must yet be accomplished before they can return to stay.

There Is More . . .

- Warped sense of time and space. Discovering time and space do not exist, losing the need to recognize measurements of life either as valid or necessary.
- Disappointment at being revived. Often feeling a need to shrink or somehow squeeze to fit back into the physical body. There can be unpleasantness, even anger or tears at the realization they are now back in their bodies and no longer on "The Other Side."

✧ ✧ ✧
What Changes Typically Occur in Children Following an NDE?

Like adults, children often show profound changes after an NDE. Common changes include:
- Altered biological patterns, such as amount of sleep, attentiveness, etc.
- Increased interest in Universal Love, rather than love of specific people
- A lessening of the parent/child bonding. The NDEr may be less demonstrative of feelings in the family. Increased sensitivity to others' feelings
- Distress from news reports and violence on TV and in movies
- Increased interest in being of service to others
- Increased interest in spirituality
- Develop a hunger for knowledge and anything philosophical which often leads to unusual choices of reading material for their age
- Often appear much more mature than children of their own age
- Difficulty relating to children of their own age
- Communication with Spirits, often labeled by children as angels or guides, and by parents as imaginary friends
- Increased sensitivity to medications, bright light, and loud noises
- A strong desire to volunteer for charitable causes

There Is More . . .

Possible changes can include:
- Increased intelligence
- Different ways of perceiving, including synesthesia (smelling color, seeing sounds, etc.)
- Increased psychic ability
- "Learning reversal" in which learning abstract concepts is easier than learning factual details (unlike most children who learn facts more easily than abstract)

Unlike adults, changes in values may not be so obvious, partly because children's values are not already well formed, and partly because they do not verbalize their values to the extent that adults do.

✧ ✧ ✧
What are the Phases of Adjustment After a Childhood NDE?

P.M.H. Atwater has suggested that children go through these five stages in the aftermath of an NDE:
1. Withdrawal and internal adjustment. In addition to the adjustment to the effects of the NDE, most children are also recovering from the physical illness or trauma that led to the NDE.
2. Realignment with friends and family; seeking ways to be of service in the world. It may be that, during this phase, up to one-third of the children get involved in the use of alcohol or drugs because of the discrepancy between the NDE and the reality of the world around them.
3. Balancing internal with external. During this time of great gain, the person is likely to develop greater self-confidence, affirm a sense of spiritual and moral values, and begin a career of service to others.
4. A time of discouragement. Sensing the disparity between their values and those of the prevailing culture, the childhood NDEr can lose heart and become depressed. It is during this time that the childhood NDEr may be prone to attempt suicide.
5. Deep integration of the NDE. During this phase, the NDEr finds the confidence to live in the world from their own perspective that is congruent with the values of the NDE.

There Is More . . .

How Can Caregivers Help a Childhood NDEr?

Caregivers play a crucial role in helping a childhood NDEr cope with the aftermath of the NDE. Following are some suggestions for caregivers to use in supporting the childhood NDEr.

- If a child has experienced a cardiac arrest, be alert to the likelihood that the child had an NDE.
- Listen, listen, listen. Be prepared to hear and show receptivity if/when a child describes near-death-like features.
- Express understanding of topics that may be difficult to discuss. These can include the child's ambivalence about returning to their body and/or the child's communication with Spirits. Trust the child's reality and respect the child's confidentiality.
- GENTLY ask open-ended questions.
- Help the child discern when and with whom it is safe to talk about their NDE-related experiences. Anticipate changes in the child.
- Be prepared to guide the child through the changes and phases of adjustment.
- Become knowledgeable about NDEs through reading, talking with NDErs, etc.
- Be prepared to support the child's increased interest in spirituality that may be expressed through increased church attendance, desire for prayer and grace, and desire for an altar in their room.
- Expect the child to initiate deep conversations about meaning and purpose in life.

- Consider encouraging the child to write and/or draw about both their NDE and adjustment process. For parents, consider keeping a journal to share with the child at a later date.
- Some characteristics and ways to respond to "highly sensitive children" may be applicable to childhood NDErs.
- Be alert for signs of significant difficulty adjusting after the NDE: withdrawal, depression, alcohol/drug abuse, and/or suicidal tendencies. In these cases, consider seeking professional help from a counselor knowledgeable about NDEs. Art and music therapy may be particularly helpful. If the child is age 2-10, play therapy may be especially appropriate.
- Participate in volunteer activities with the child if you are their parent.
- Teach them visualization techniques so that they can revisit pleasurable aspects of the NDE (without the physical circumstances that accompanied it).

There Is More . . .

Support and Resources for NDEs, dNDEs, OBEs and STEs

IANDS
International Association of Near-Death Studies
2741 Campus Walk Avenue
Building 500
Durham, NC 27705-8878
919-383-7940 (voice and fax)
Iands.org

The International Association for Near-Death Studies (IANDS) is the only membership organization in the world devoted exclusively to providing information about near-death and related experiences to experiencers, researchers, educators, healthcare providers, and the interested public.

In addition to maintaining its information-rich website, IANDS publishes a peer-reviewed scholarly journal and a member newsletter, sponsors conferences and other programs, works with the media, and encourages the formation of regional discussion and support groups. We invite you to join and become part of this mission, and keep up to date on what is known about this fascinating subject.

To find IANDS chapters near you, visit iands.org.

Support Resources

ACISTE
American Center for the Integration of
Spiritual Transformative Experiences (STEs)

P.O. Box 1472
Alpine, CA 91903
Info@Aciste.org
Aciste.org

What is a spiritually transformative experience or STE?

An experience is spiritually transformative when it causes people to perceive themselves and the world profoundly differently: by expanding the individual's identity, augmenting their sensitivities, and thereby altering their values, priorities and appreciation of the purpose of life. This may be triggered by surviving clinical death, or by otherwise sensing an enlarged reality.

ACISTE offers research, education and support. Their programs include the following:

- ➢ Guides experiencers to venues for support, sharing, discussion, networking and care.

- ➢ Sponsors forums where experiencers can further explore, develop, and share their experiences and implications with others.

- ➢ Provides resources to experiencers, their families, and others involved in their lives for further understanding and support.

There Is More . . .

➢ Educates first-responders, medical professionals and other caregivers in identifying and supporting the experiencer initially. They offer first-responders and professional caregivers regularly-updated resources for referring experiencers to appropriately trained professionals and supportive programs.

➢ Conducts and fosters research to continually increase understanding of the integration process and to develop even more effective tools in supporting experiencers.

➢ Supports research of spiritually transformative experiences as potential catalysts for health and wellness of society as a whole.

✧ ✧ ✧
OTHER SUPPORT AND RESOURCES

ABUSE

Childhelp USA® National Child Abuse Hotline
1-800-4-A-CHILD® (1-800-422-4453)
Hours: 24 hours a day, 7 days a week
Serving the United States, Canada, U.S. Virgin Islands, Puerto Rico, and Guam.
Offers three-way calling and communication in 140 languages.
childhelpusa.org

Elder or Dependent Adult Abuse Hotline
888-436-3600

National Center for Victims of Crime Helpline
1-800-394-2255 or TTY: 1-800-211-7996
Serving victims in more than 150 languages.
Hours: Monday through Friday, 8:30 am – 8:30 pm (Eastern Time)
ncvc.org

National Coalition Against Domestic Violence Hotline
800-799-7233 or TTY 800-787-3224
Hours: 24 hours a day, 7 days a week
Se Hablo Espanol
ncadv.org

Prevent Child Abuse America
312-663-3520
Hours: 9:00 am – 5:00 pm, Monday-Friday (Central Time)
preventchildabuse.org

There Is More . . .

Rape Abuse and Incest National Network (RAINN)
1-800-656-Hope or 1-800-656- 4673
TTY: 1-800-810-7440
Hours: 24 hours a day, 7 days a week
rainn.org

ADDICTIONS

AL ANON (and **ALATEEN** for younger members):
1-800-4AL-ANON (1-888-425-2666), in Canada and the USA
Hours: Monday through Friday 8:00 am to 6:00 pm
(Eastern Time)
A worldwide organization offering a self-help recovery program for families and friends of alcoholics whether or not the alcoholic seeks help or even recognizes the existence of a drinking problem.

Alcoholics Anonymous (AA)
General Service Office
475 Riverside Drive, 11th Floor
New York, NY 10115
212-870-3400
Hours: 8:30 am - 4:45 pm, Monday-Friday (Eastern Time)
Alcoholics Anonymous groups can be found in the white pages of your local phone book.
alcoholics-anoymous.org

Children of Alcoholics Foundation
coaf.org

Cocaine Anonymous
National referral line: 1-800-347-8998

Other Support and Resources

National Council on Alcoholism and Drug Dependence Helpline
1-800-622-2255
Counseling and treatment.
Enter your zip code to find a location near you.
ncadd.org

National Institute of Drug Abuse (NIDA)
301-443-6245
800-662-4357 Treatment Referral Routing Center
Hours: Monday through Friday 8:30 am – 5:00 pm
(Eastern Time)
drugabuse.gov

Nar-Anon Family Group Headquarters, Inc.
22527 Crenshaw Blvd #200B
Torrance, CA 90505 USA
310-534-8188 or 800-477-6291
FAX 310-534-8688
Twelve-step, self-help program for family, friends, and loved ones of someone who has a narcotic problem.

Narcotics Anonymous
1-818-773-9999
Hours: Monday through Friday 8:00 am to 5:00 pm
na.org

Overeaters Anonymous
505-891-2664
oa.org

There Is More . . .

ORGANIZATIONS

American Cancer Society
1-800-227-2345
Hours: 24 hours a day, 7 days a week

American Diabetes Association
1-800-342-2383
Hours: Monday through Friday 8:30 am – 8:00 pm
(Eastern Time)

American Heart Association
1-800-242-8721
Hours: 24 hours a day, 7 days a week

American Lung Association
Lung Help Line 1-800-548-8252
to speak with a health care professional.
On the website, enter your zip code to find a chapter near you.
lungusa.org

Mothers Against Drunk Drivers (MADD)
800-GET-MADD, (800-438-6233)
Hours: Monday through Friday 8:00 am – 5:00 pm
madd.org

National Cancer Institute
800-4-CANCER (800-422-6227)
nci.nih.gov

Other Support and Resources

National Hospice and Palliative Care Organization
703-837-1500
Hours: Monday through Friday, 9:00 am – 6:00 pm
(Eastern Time)
nhpco.org

EATING DISORDERS

**National Association of Anorexia Nervosa
and Associated Disorders**
1-847-831-3438
Monday through Friday, 9:00 am to 5 pm
(Central Time)
anad.org

National Eating Disorders Association
603 Stewart Street, Suite 803
Seattle, WA 98101
1-800-931-2237
Hours: Monday through Friday, 8:30 am to 4:30 pm
(Pacific Time)
After hours, leave a message and someone will return your call
as soon as possible.

EMOTIONAL RESILIENCE
CorStone
415-331-6161
CorStone (formerly, the International Center for
Attitudinal Healing) develops and supports
emotional resilience in children, families, and
communities to better deal with
challenge, conflict, or crisis.

There Is More . . .

The organization provides comprehensive trainings and
facilitated peer support group services
around the world in the areas of:
aging, bereavement, HIV/AIDS, family resilience,
and children and youth conflict management programs.
CorStone's approach and philosophy is based on
universal values and the importance of embracing a
positive attitude, love, and forgiveness as the
means toward making peaceful
and healthful choices.
corstone.org

AIDS INFO
1-800-HIV-0440 (1-800-448-0440)
TTY: 1-888-480-3739
International: 1-301-519-0459
Fax: 1-301-519-6616
Hours: Monday through Friday 12:00 pm to 5:00 pm
(Eastern Time)
Chat room: Aidsinfo.nih.gov/livehelp
12:00 pm to 4:00 pm, Monday through Friday
E-mail: contactus@aidsinfo.nih.gov
Callers can speak with experienced health specialists for
information about approved HIV treatment and help in locating
HIV/AIDS clinical trials across the USA.
In English, en Español.

SUICIDE
American Association of Suicidology
5221 Wisconsin Avenue, NW
Washington, DC 20015
Phone: (202) 237-2280
Fax: (202) 237-2282

Other Support and Resources

Email: info@suicidology.org
Education and resources.
suicidology.org

The National Suicide Prevention Lifeline
1-800-273-TALK 1-800-273-8255
Access to trained telephone counselors,
24 hours a day, 7 days a week.

The Samaritans Suicide Prevention Hotline
1-212-673-3000
Hours: 24 hours a day, 7 days a week
Suicide crisis hotline.

Suicide Life Line Hotline
1-800-SUICIDE (1-800-784-2433)
Hours: 24 hours a day, 7 days a week

TEENS

Teens Drug and Alcohol - Free Vibe
Teen approach to peer pressure, anti-drug message, and the media. Personal stories, online games, and message boards. Freevibe is the site for teens to get scientifically accurate drug information, games, and tips for leading
healthy lifestyles and rejecting drugs.
freevibe.com

The Safe Space
The safe place, a project to break the cycle, is the most comprehensive resource on the web where teens and young adults can learn about domestic and dating violence, as well as their legal rights and options.
thesafespace.org

Recommended Books by International Association of Near-Death Studies (IANDS)

Because of the large variety of books on the subject of NDEs, I asked Diane Corcoran, RN, PhD, president of IANDS to share a few that she feels will be helpful.

P.M.H. Atwater, LHD PhD, is well known in the field of NDEs and children with NDEs.

P.M.H. Atwater—*The New Children and Near-Death Experiences*

P.M.H. Atwater—*Beyond the Indigo Children: The New Children and the Coming of the Fifth World*

P.M.H. Atwater—*Beyond the Light: What Isn't Being Said About Near-Death Experiences: from Visions of Heaven to Glimpses of Hell*

P.M.H. Atwater—*We Live Forever: The Real Truth about Death*

P.M.H Atwater—*Future Memory*

P.M.H. Atwater—*Coming Back to Life: Examining the After-Effects of the Near-Death Experience*

P.M.H. Atwater—*The Big Book of Near-Death Experiences: The Ultimate Guide to What Happens When We Die*

P.M.H. Atwater, and David H. Morgan—*The Complete Idiot's Guide to Near-Death Experiences*

Maggie Callanan and Patricia Kelley write about approaching death.

Maggie Callanan and Patricia Kelley—*Final Gift: Understanding the Special Awareness, Needs, and Communications of the Dying* and *Final Journey*

Maggie Callanan—*Final Journeys: A Practical Guide for Bringing Care and Comfort at the End of Life*

Raymond A. Moody was one of the first people to bring about the awareness of NDEs and what to call them.

Raymond A. Moody—*The Light Beyond*

Raymond A. Moody—*Life After Life: The Investigation of a Phenomenon—Survival of Bodily Death*

Raymond A. Moody—*Life After Life and Reflections on Life After Life: A Guideposts 2 in 1 Book*

Raymond A. Moody and James R. Lewis—*The Death and Afterlife Book: The Encyclopedia of Death, Near Death, and Life After Death*

Barbara Rommer, MD—her book is about frightening or distressing NDEs.

Barbara Rommer, MD—*Blessing in Disguise: Another Side of the Near-Death Experience*

✧ ✧ ✧
Other Valuable Books and DVDs

Recommended by Sharon Lund, DD

Aron, Elaine N., PhD. *The Highly Sensitive Person: How to Thrive When the World Overwhelms You*

Beckwith, Michael Bernard. *Spiritual Liberation: Fulfilling Your Soul's Purpose*

Dossey, Larry, Dr. *The Power of Premonitions: How Knowing the Future Shapes Our Lives*

Gawain, Shakti. *Living in the Light: A Guide to Personal and Planetary Transformation*

Kübler-Ross, Elisabeth and Myss, Caroline. *On Life after Death, revised*

Kübler-Ross, Elisabeth. *On Death and Dying*

Kübler-Ross, Elisabeth and Kessler, David. *On Grief and Grieving: Finding the Meaning of Grief Through the Five Stages of Loss*

Levine, Stephen and Ondrea. *A Year to Live: How to Live This Year as If It Were Your Last*

Levine, Stephen and Ondrea. *Unattended Sorrows: Recovering from Loss and Reviving the Heart*

Other Valuable Books and DVDs

Levine, Stephen and Ondrea. *Who Dies?: An Investigation of Conscious Living and Conscious Dying*

Long, Jeffrey, MD and Perry, Paul. *Evidence of the Afterlife: The Science of Near-Death Experiences*

Long, Jody, JD. *From Soul to Soulmate: Bridges from Near-Death Experience Wisdom*

Lund, Sharon, DD. *Sacred Living, Sacred Dying: A Guide to Embracing Life and Death*

Lund, Sharon, DD. *The Integrated Being: Techniques to Heal Your Mind-Body-Spirit*

MacLeod, Ainslie. *The Instruction: Living the Life Your Soul Intended*

McWilliams, Peter, Bloomfield, Harold H., and Colgrove, Melba. *How to Survive the Loss of A Love*

Siegel, Bernie S., MD. *Love, Medicine and Miracles*

Tipping, Colin C. *Radical Forgiveness: Making Room for the Miracles*

Weiss, Brian L. *Many Lives, Many Masters: The True Story of a Prominent Psychiatrist, His Young Patient, and the Past-Life Therapy that Changed Both Their Lives*

DVD/Documentaries (both available through SacredLife.com)

Dying to LIVE: NDE

Mustang Man: How a Wild Horse Tamed a Vietnam Vet

www.ingramcontent.com/pod-product-compliance
Lightning Source LLC
Chambersburg PA
CBHW061306110426
42742CB00012BA/2078